3 Ingredient
cookbook

Contents

Mojito Shrimp Cocktail

1 pound frozen medium raw shrimp, deveined but not peeled
1 cup plus 2 tablespoons prepared mojito cocktail mix, divided
2 tablespoons olive oil
1 jar shrimp cocktail sauce

1. Place frozen shrimp in large shallow glass dish. Pour 1 cup mojito mix over shrimp to cover. (Separate shrimp as much as possible to aid thawing.) Marinate in refrigerator 10 to 24 hours or until thawed, stirring shrimp once or twice.

2. Prepare grill for direct cooking.* Drain shrimp; discard marinade. *Do not peel.* Pat dry and place in large bowl with oil; toss to coat.

3. Grill shrimp over medium-high heat 10 to 15 minutes or until pink and opaque, turning once. Refrigerate until ready to serve.

4. Pour cocktail sauce into serving bowl; add remaining 1 to 2 tablespoons mojito mix and stir to combine. Peel shrimp before serving or provide bowl for shells.   *Makes 6 to 8 servings*

Shrimp may also be cooked in grill pan.

Add fresh chopped mint to the cocktail sauce instead of, or in addition to, the mojito mix. Serve with lime wedges.

BBQ Orange Wings

8 TYSON® Individually Frozen Chicken Wings
½ cup bottled barbecue sauce
½ cup orange marmalade or plum or pineapple preserves
Salt and black pepper to taste

1. Preheat oven to 400°F. Line 13×9-inch baking pan with foil; spray with nonstick cooking spray. Wash hands. Arrange frozen wings in single layer in pan. Wash hands. Combine barbecue sauce and marmalade; reserve half of mixture to serve with cooked wings.

2. Bake wings 20 minutes; drain and discard juices. Sprinkle wings with salt and pepper. Bake an additional 20 minutes. Turn over wings and baste with sauce. Bake 15 to 20 minutes more or until internal juices of chicken run clear. (Or insert instant-read meat thermometer into thickest part of chicken. Temperature should read 180°F.)

3. Heat reserved sauce and serve with wings. Refrigerate leftovers immediately. *Makes 4 servings*

Prep Time: 5 minutes • **Cook Time:** 1 hour

Spinach, Artichoke & Feta Dip

½ cup thawed frozen chopped spinach
1 cup crumbled feta cheese
½ teaspoon black pepper
1 cup marinated artichokes, undrained

1. Place spinach in small microwavable bowl; microwave on HIGH 2 minutes.

2. Place feta and pepper in food processor; process 1 minute or until finely chopped. Add artichokes and spinach; process 30 seconds or until well mixed but not puréed.

Makes about 1½ cups

Serving Suggestion: Serve with pita chips or crackers.

Goat Cheese-Stuffed Figs

7 fresh firm ripe figs
7 slices prosciutto
1 package (4 ounces) goat cheese
Ground black pepper

1. Preheat broiler. Line baking sheet or broiler pan with foil. Cut figs in half vertically. Cut prosciutto slices in half to create 14 pieces (about 4 inches long and 1 inch wide).

2. Spread 1 teaspoon goat cheese onto cut side of each fig half. Wrap prosciutto slice around fig and goat cheese. Sprinkle with pepper.

3. Broil about 4 minutes or until cheese softens and figs are heated through. *Makes 4 to 6 servings*

Pesto Terrine

1 package (8 ounces) cream cheese, softened, divided
2 tablespoons butter, softened, divided
5 tablespoons basil pesto, divided
4 tablespoons sun-dried tomato pesto

1. Line 1- to 1½-cup bowl or mold with plastic wrap. Allow edges of wrap to extend over side of bowl.

2. Place half of cream cheese, 1 tablespoon butter and 4 tablespoons basil pesto in food processor. Pulse until well blended, scraping down side of bowl frequently. Transfer mixture to prepared bowl; press down firmly. Gently spread remaining 1 tablespoon basil pesto on top of mixture. (Drain as much oil as possible from pesto to avoid greasiness.)

3. Place remaining half of cream cheese, 1 tablespoon butter and sun-dried tomato pesto in clean bowl of food processor. Pulse until completely combined, scraping down side of bowl frequently. Press tomato mixture down firmly on top of basil pesto, smoothing top. Cover and refrigerate terrine at least 1 hour.

4. To serve, place small plate on top of bowl, invert bowl and use plastic wrap to ease terrine out of bowl. Smooth surface with knife and blot excess oil with paper towel. Serve terrine with crackers or toasts. *Makes 6 to 8 servings*

Ham & Swiss Twists

1 package (about 13 ounces) refrigerated pizza dough
6 very thin slices Swiss cheese
6 very thin slices smoked ham
Black pepper

1. Preheat oven to 400°F. Line baking sheets with parchment paper.

2. Unroll dough on cutting board or clean work surface; press into 16×12-inch rectangle. Arrange single layer of cheese slices over half of dough, cutting slices to fit as necessary. Top with ham slices; sprinkle with pepper. Fold remaining half of dough over ham and cheese layers, creating 12×8-inch rectangle.

3. Cut dough into ½-inch strips (8 inches long). Twist strips several times; place on prepared baking sheets. Bake about 14 minutes or until golden brown. Serve warm. *Makes about 22 twists*

Tip: For extra flavor, spread honey or Dijon mustard over dough before layering with cheese and ham. Serve with additional mustard for dipping.

Salsa-Style Wings

1½ pounds chicken wings
2 cups prepared salsa
¼ cup brown sugar

1. Preheat oven to 350°F. Line 13×9-inch baking pan with foil. Place chicken in even layer on bottom of pan.

2. Stir salsa and brown sugar in medium bowl until blended; pour over chicken.

3. Bake 1 hour or until chicken is cooked through, basting every 10 minutes with salsa mixture from pan. Serve with remaining salsa mixture. *Makes 4 to 6 servings*

Apricot Brie en Croûte

1 sheet frozen puff pastry (half of 17¼-ounce package), thawed
1 round (8 ounces) Brie cheese
¼ cup apricot preserves

1. Preheat oven to 400°F. Line baking sheet with parchment paper.

2. Roll out pastry sheet on lightly floured surface into 12-inch square. Place Brie in center of square; spread preserves over top of Brie.

3. Gather up edges of pastry sheet and bring together over center of Brie, covering cheese entirely. Pinch and twist pastry edges together to seal. Transfer to prepared baking sheet.

4. Bake 20 to 25 minutes or until golden brown. (If top of pastry browns too quickly, cover loosely with small piece of foil.) Serve warm. *Makes 6 servings*

Tips: For added flavor and texture, sprinkle 2 tablespoons sliced almonds over the preserves. Proceed with wrapping and baking the Brie as directed. Serve with crackers or bread.

Mini Swiss Quiches

4 eggs
¼ teaspoon *each* salt and black pepper
¾ cup (3 ounces) shredded Swiss cheese
1 unbaked 9-inch pie crust

1. Preheat oven to 300°F. Spray 20 mini (1¾-inch) muffin cups with nonstick cooking spray.

2. Whisk eggs, salt and pepper in medium bowl; stir in cheese.

3. Roll out pie crust into 13-inch circle. Cut dough with 3-inch round biscuit cutter. Gather and reroll scraps to make 20 circles. Press circles into prepared muffin cups. Fill cups with egg mixture.

4. Bake 30 minutes or until tops are puffy and toothpick inserted into centers comes out clean. *Makes 20 quiches*

Smoked Salmon Omelet Roll-Ups

4 eggs
⅛ teaspoon black pepper
¼ cup chive and onion cream cheese, softened
1 package (about 4 ounces) smoked salmon, cut into bite-size pieces

1. Beat eggs and pepper in small bowl until well blended (no streaks of white showing). Spray large nonstick skillet with nonstick cooking spray; heat over medium-high heat.

2. Pour half of egg mixture into skillet; tilt skillet to completely coat bottom with thin layer of eggs. Cook, without stirring, 2 to 4 minutes or until eggs are set. Use spatula to carefully loosen omelet from skillet; slide onto cutting board. Repeat with remaining egg mixture to make second omelet.

3. Spread 2 tablespoons cream cheese over each omelet; top with smoked salmon pieces. Roll up omelets tightly; wrap in plastic wrap and refrigerate at least 30 minutes. Cut off ends, then cut rolls crosswise into ½-inch slices.   *Makes about 24 pieces*

Roasted Red Pepper Dip

8 ounces reduced-fat cream cheese, softened
½ cup roasted red peppers, from a bottle, well drained
2 tablespoons MRS. DASH® Garlic & Herb Seasoning Blend
2 tablespoons olive oil

1. Combine cream cheese, red peppers, MRS. DASH® Garlic & Herb Seasoning Blend and olive oil in a blender or food processor.

2. Blend or process until smooth.

3. Chill 1 to 2 hours.

4. Serve with crackers, tortilla chips or vegetables.
Makes 8 servings

Prep Time: 5 minutes

Lamb-Sicles

 6 cloves garlic
 1 teaspoon salt
 2 tablespoons finely chopped fresh rosemary leaves
 2 tablespoons olive oil
 ½ teaspoon black pepper
12 small lamb rib chops, bone-in and frenched*

*The term "frenched" means that the fat and meat have been cut away from the end of the bone protruding from the chop. Ask the butcher to do this for you if frenched chops are not available already cut. You can also purchase a frenched rack of lamb and cut it into individual chops.

1. Chop garlic with salt until finely minced. Place in small bowl; add rosemary, oil and pepper. Mix well.

2. Rub mixture on both sides of chops; wrap in single layer in foil and refrigerate 30 minutes to 3 hours.

3. Prepare grill for direct cooking or preheat broiler. Grill chops on well-oiled grid over medium-high heat 2 to 5 minutes per side or until medium-rare (145°F). Lamb should feel slightly firm when pressed. (To check doneness, cut small slit in meat near bone; lamb should be rosy pink.) *Makes 4 servings*

Tips: Add 2 teaspoons Dijon mustard to the marinade. Serve the lamb with mint jelly.

Crispy Bacon Sticks

½ cup (1½ ounces) grated Wisconsin Parmesan cheese, divided
 5 slices bacon, halved lengthwise
10 breadsticks

Microwave Directions

Spread ¼ cup cheese on plate. Press one side of bacon into cheese; wrap diagonally around breadstick with cheese-coated side toward stick. Place on paper plate or microwave-safe baking sheet lined with paper towels. Repeat with remaining bacon halves, cheese and breadsticks. Microwave on HIGH 4 to 6 minutes or until bacon is cooked, checking for doneness after 4 minutes. Roll again in remaining ¼ cup Parmesan cheese. Serve warm.
 Makes 10 sticks

*Favorite recipe from **Wisconsin Milk Marketing Board***

Pesto Scallop Skewers

1 to 2 red or yellow bell peppers, cut into bite-size pieces
16 jumbo sea scallops (about 1 pound)
2 tablespoons pesto

1. Thread 2 bell pepper pieces and 1 scallop onto each of 16 short wooden skewers. Brush pesto over peppers and scallops.

2. Heat nonstick grill pan or large nonstick skillet over medium-high heat. Cook skewers 2 to 3 minutes on each side or until scallops are opaque in center. *Makes 16 appetizers*

Caprese Pizza

1 loaf (1 pound) frozen pizza or bread dough, thawed
1 container (12 ounces) bruschetta sauce
1 container (8 ounces) pearl-size fresh mozzarella cheese (perlini), drained*

*If pearl-size mozzarella is not available, use one 8-ounce ball of fresh mozzarella and chop into 1/4-inch pieces.

1. Preheat oven to 400°F. Spray jelly-roll pan or baking sheet with nonstick cooking spray.

2. Roll out dough on lightly floured surface into 15×10-inch rectangle. Transfer to prepared pan. Cover loosely with plastic wrap; let rest 10 minutes. Meanwhile, place bruschetta sauce in colander; let drain 10 minutes.

3. Prick surface of dough several times with fork. Bake 10 minutes. Sprinkle with drained bruschetta sauce and top with mozzarella. Bake 10 minutes or until cheese is melted and crust is golden brown. Serve warm. *Makes 6 servings*

Note: Bruschetta sauce is a mixture of diced fresh tomatoes, garlic, basil and olive oil. It is typically found in the refrigerated section of the supermarket with other prepared dips.

Spicy Almond Chicken Wings

3 pounds chicken drummettes
2 tablespoons jerk seasoning
2 tablespoons vegetable oil
½ teaspoon salt
1 cup slivered almonds, finely chopped

1. Place drummettes in large bowl. Add jerk seasoning, oil and salt; toss to coat. Cover and refrigerate 20 to 30 minutes.

2. Preheat oven to 400°F. Line large shallow baking pan with foil. Spray with nonstick cooking spray.

3. Place almonds in shallow bowl. Roll drummettes in almonds until coated. Place in prepared baking pan. Bake 30 to 35 minutes or until chicken is cooked through.   *Makes 8 to 10 servings*

Bacon-Wrapped Teriyaki Shrimp

1 pound large raw shrimp, peeled and deveined (with tails on)
¼ cup teriyaki marinade
11 to 12 slices bacon

1. Preheat oven to 425°F. Line shallow baking pan with foil.

2. Place shrimp in large resealable food storage bag. Add marinade; seal bag. Turn bag to coat shrimp. Marinate in refrigerator 15 to 20 minutes.

3. Meanwhile, separate bacon slices; cut in half crosswise.

4. Remove shrimp from bag, reserving marinade. Wrap each shrimp with 1 piece of bacon. Place shrimp in prepared baking pan; brush bacon with some of reserved marinade. Bake 15 minutes or until shrimp are pink and opaque.
Makes 4 to 5 servings

Tip: Do not use thick-cut bacon for this recipe, because the bacon will not be completely cooked when the shrimp are done.

1-2-3 Guacamole

  2 ripe avocados
  4 green onions, chopped
  2 tablespoons lime juice
  ¼ teaspoon salt
  ⅛ teaspoon black pepper

1. Cut avocados in half; remove and discard pits. Scoop avocado flesh from skins and place in medium bowl. Mash with fork.

2. Add green onions, lime juice, salt and pepper; stir until blended. Transfer to serving bowl. Serve immediately.   *Makes 6 servings*

Tips: Add 1 or 2 chopped seeded plum tomatoes in step 2. Serve with tortilla chips.

Warm Goat Cheese Rounds

  1 package (4 ounces) goat cheese
  1 egg
  1 tablespoon water
  ⅓ cup seasoned bread crumbs

1. Cut goat cheese crosswise into 8 (¼-inch-thick) slices. (If cheese is too difficult to slice, shape scant tablespoonfuls of cheese into balls and flatten into ¼-inch-thick rounds.)

2. Beat egg and water in small bowl. Place bread crumbs in shallow dish. Dip goat cheese rounds in egg mixture, then in bread crumbs, turning to coat all sides. Gently press bread crumbs to adhere. Place coated rounds on plate; freeze 10 minutes.

3. Cook goat cheese rounds in medium nonstick skillet over medium-high heat about 2 minutes per side or until golden brown. Serve immediately.   *Makes 4 servings*

Serving Suggestions: Serve with heated marinara sauce or over mixed greens tossed with vinaigrette dressing.

Pork Tenderloin Roast
with Fig Sauce

1 tablespoon olive oil
1 pork tenderloin roast (about 1 pound)
1 teaspoon salt
½ teaspoon black pepper
1 jar (about 8 ounces) fig jam or preserves
¼ cup dry red wine

1. Preheat oven to 375°F. Heat oil in large skillet over medium heat. Brown pork on all sides. Sprinkle with salt and pepper; place in shallow roasting pan. Roast 15 minutes.

2. Meanwhile, combine fig jam and wine in same skillet. Cook and stir over low heat 5 minutes or until melted and warm.

3. Brush small amount of fig sauce over pork. Roast 5 to 10 minutes or until temperature reaches 155°F on instant-read thermometer. Transfer pork to cutting board. Tent with foil; let stand 10 minutes.

4. Cut pork into thin slices. Serve with remaining fig sauce.

Makes 4 servings

Tip: For extra flavor, combine 2 cloves minced garlic, 1 teaspoon coarse salt, 1 teaspoon dried rosemary and ¼ teaspoon red pepper flakes in a small bowl. Brush over the pork after browning.

Grilled Picante BBQ Chicken

¾ cup PACE® Picante Sauce
¼ cup barbecue sauce
6 skinless, boneless chicken breast halves

1. Stir the picante sauce and barbecue sauce in a small bowl. Reserve ½ **cup** picante sauce mixture for grilling. Set aside remaining picante sauce mixture to serve with the chicken.

2. Lightly oil the grill rack and heat the grill to medium. Grill the chicken for 15 minutes or until it's cooked through, turning and brushing often with the reserved picante sauce mixture during grilling. Discard any remaining picante sauce mixture.

3. Serve the chicken with the remaining ½ **cup** picante sauce mixture. *Makes 6 servings*

Tip: This simple basting sauce also makes a zesty dipping sauce for chicken wings or nuggets.

Prep Time: 5 minutes • **Cook Time:** 15 minutes

Turkey Breast with Honey-Mustard Glaze

1 turkey breast (4 to 6 pounds), fresh or thawed
½ teaspoon salt
¼ teaspoon black pepper
¼ cup honey
2 tablespoons Dijon mustard

1. Preheat oven to 325°F. Season all sides of turkey breast with salt and pepper.

2. Place turkey on V-shaped rack in small roasting pan. Roast, uncovered, 1½ to 2¼ hours or until temperature reaches 165°F in thickest part of breast.

3. Meanwhile, combine honey and mustard in small bowl. Brush glaze over turkey during last 20 minutes of cooking. Cover and let turkey stand 10 minutes before slicing. *Makes 10 servings*

Italian Sausage Sandwiches

1 pound Italian pork sausage, casing removed
**1½ cups PREGO® Chunky Garden Mushroom & Green Pepper
     Italian Sauce**
4 long hard rolls, split

1. Cook the sausage in a 10-inch skillet over medium-high heat until it's well browned, stirring often to separate meat. Pour off any fat.

2. Stir in the sauce and cook until the mixture is hot and bubbling. Serve the sausage mixture on the rolls.   *Makes 4 sandwiches*

Kitchen Tip: You can use your favorite PREGO® Italian Sauce in this recipe.

Prep Time: 5 minutes • **Cook Time:** 15 minutes

Jambalaya in a Jiffy

2 tablespoons olive oil, divided
**2 links (6 ounces) andouille or smoked sausage, cut into
     ¼-inch slices**
**8 ounces boneless skinless chicken thighs or breasts, cut
     into ½-inch pieces**
2½ cups water
1 package (8 ounces) jambalaya rice mix

1. Heat 1 tablespoon oil in large skillet over medium-high heat. Add sausage; cook about 6 minutes or until browned, stirring occasionally. Push sausage to side of skillet. Add remaining 1 tablespoon oil and chicken to skillet; cook and stir about 5 minutes or until lightly browned.

2. Meanwhile, bring water to a boil in medium saucepan over high heat. Add rice mix; bring to a boil. Reduce heat to low; cover and simmer 10 minutes.

3. Stir sausage and chicken into rice. Cover and simmer 15 minutes or until water is absorbed. Fluff rice with fork before serving.   *Makes 4 servings*

Chicken with Herb Stuffing

⅓ **cup fresh basil leaves**
1 **package (8 ounces) goat cheese with garlic and herbs**
4 **boneless skinless chicken breasts**
1 **to 2 tablespoons olive oil**

1. Place basil in food processor; process with on/off pulses until chopped. Cut goat cheese into large pieces and add to food processor; process with on/off pulses until combined.

2. Preheat oven to 350°F. Place 1 chicken breast on cutting board and cover with plastic wrap. Pound to ¼-inch thickness with meat mallet. Repeat with remaining chicken.

3. Shape about 2 tablespoons of cheese mixture into log; place in center of each chicken breast. Roll chicken around filling to enclose completely. Tie securely with kitchen twine.

4. Heat 1 tablespoon oil in large ovenproof skillet. Brown chicken bundles on all sides, adding additional oil as needed to prevent sticking. Place skillet in oven; bake 15 minutes or until chicken is cooked through and filling is hot. Allow to cool slightly before removing twine and slicing. *Makes 4 servings*

One-Pan Italian

1 **package (approximately 1 pound) JOHNSONVILLE® Italian Sausage Links, casings removed or 1 package JOHNSONVILLE® Italian Ground Sausage**
1 **jar (26 ounces) favorite pasta sauce**
3 **cups water**
8 **ounces uncooked spaghetti, broken in half**

In a large skillet, place sausage, breaking into bite-sized pieces. Cook over medium heat until browned and no longer pink; drain. Add pasta sauce and water; bring to a boil.

Add spaghetti. Simmer, uncovered, for 8 to 10 minutes or until spaghetti is tender, stirring often. *Makes 5 servings*

Onion-Wine Pot Roast

2 tablespoons olive oil, divided
1 teaspoon salt, divided
½ teaspoon black pepper
1 boneless beef chuck roast (about 3 pounds), trimmed
2 pounds yellow onions, cut in half and thinly sliced
2 tablespoons water
2 cups red wine, such as cabernet sauvignon or merlot

1. Heat 1 tablespoon oil in Dutch oven over medium-high heat. Sprinkle ½ teaspoon salt and pepper over beef; place in Dutch oven. Cook until beef is well browned on both sides, about 6 minutes per side. Remove beef to large plate.

2. Preheat oven to 300°F. Add remaining 1 tablespoon oil, onions and ½ teaspoon salt to Dutch oven; cook over medium-high heat 10 minutes, stirring frequently. Stir in water, scraping up any browned bits from bottom of Dutch oven. Reduce heat to medium; partially cover and cook 15 minutes or until onions are deep golden brown, stirring occasionally.

3. Stir in wine. Return beef to Dutch oven with any accumulated juices. Cover and bake about 3 hours or until beef is fork-tender.

4. Remove beef from Dutch oven; keep warm. Skim fat from juices; serve with beef. *Makes 6 servings*

Serving Suggestion: Serve pot roast with mashed potatoes or hot cooked orzo pasta.

Crispy Onion Chicken

1½ cups *French's*® French Fried Onions
¼ cup *French's*® Honey Dijon Mustard or *French's*® Honey Mustard
6 boneless skinless chicken breast halves

1. Heat oven to 400°F. Crush French Fried Onions in plastic bag with hands or rolling pin. Transfer to sheet of waxed paper.

2. Spread mustard evenly on chicken. Coat with onion crumbs, pressing gently to adhere.

3. Place in baking pan. Bake 20 minutes or until chicken is no longer pink in center. *Makes 6 servings*

Hot Sweet Mustard Chicken

4 cups small pretzel twists
8 boneless skinless chicken thighs* (about 2 pounds)
Salt and black pepper
½ cup hot sweet mustard

*Boneless skinless chicken breasts can also be used; reduce cooking time to 20 to 25 minutes.

1. Preheat oven to 350°F. Line baking sheet with foil; place wire rack over foil and spray with nonstick cooking spray.

2. Place pretzels in large resealable food storage bag; seal bag. Crush pretzels with rolling pin, meat mallet or heavy skillet. (Pretzels should yield about 2 cups crumbs.) Place pretzel crumbs in shallow dish.

3. Season chicken with salt and pepper. Generously brush both sides of chicken with mustard; coat with pretzel crumbs, pressing crumbs into mustard to adhere. Place chicken on prepared rack.

4. Bake 35 to 40 minutes or until chicken is cooked through.

Makes 4 to 6 servings

Pork & Asparagus Stir-Fry

¾ pound pork tenderloin
3 tablespoons Chinese black bean sauce
½ teaspoon black pepper
¾ pound asparagus (25 to 30 spears), cut into bite-size pieces
2 to 3 tablespoons water

1. Trim pork and cut into bite-size pieces. Heat large nonstick skillet or wok over medium-high heat. Add pork, black bean sauce and pepper; stir-fry 5 minutes or until pork is browned.

2. Add asparagus and water to skillet; stir-fry until pork is cooked through and asparagus is crisp-tender, adding additional water if needed to prevent sticking.

Makes 4 servings

Tips: Add red or green bell pepper strips with the asparagus. Serve the stir-fry over rice or noodles. Garnish with chopped green onions.

Spicy Shrimp Sauté

2 tablespoons butter
1 pound shrimp, peeled,* deveined
½ cup ORTEGA® Taco Sauce
½ cup ORTEGA® Salsa con Queso

*For easier handling and an attractive appearance, leave tails on.

Melt butter over medium heat in large skillet. Add shrimp; stir to coat with butter. Cook and stir 5 minutes or until shrimp turn pink.

Add taco sauce; stir to coat well. Cook 4 minutes or until sauce has thickened.

Microwave salsa on HIGH (100% power) for 30 seconds to warm. Serve with shrimp. *Makes 4 servings*

Tip: For an innovative appetizer, replace the shrimp with sea scallops; serve the scallops on toothpicks.

Tip: To devein shrimp, make a small cut along the back and lift out the dark vein with the tip of a knife. You may find this easier to do under cold running water.

Prep Time: 5 minutes • **Start to Finish Time:** 15 minutes

Pork Chops with Creamy Mustard Sauce

4 center-cut pork chops (¾ inch thick)
Salt and black pepper
⅓ cup water
½ cup coarse-grain mustard
¼ cup whipping cream

1. Season pork chops with salt and pepper. Spray large skillet with nonstick cooking spray; heat over medium heat. Cook pork about 10 minutes or until barely pink in center, turning once. Remove from skillet; keep warm.

2. For sauce, add water to skillet; bring to a boil, scraping up browned bits from bottom of skillet. Reduce heat; simmer 1 to 2 minutes. Add mustard and cream; cook and stir just until sauce begins to simmer. Serve over pork chops. *Makes 4 servings*

Honey-Roasted Chicken and Butternut Squash

1 pound fresh butternut squash chunks
Salt and black pepper
6 bone-in chicken thighs
2 tablespoons honey

1. Preheat oven to 375°F. Spray baking sheet and wire rack with nonstick cooking spray.

2. Spread squash on prepared baking sheet; season with salt and pepper. Place wire rack over squash; arrange chicken on rack. Season with salt and pepper.

3. Roast 25 minutes. Carefully lift rack and stir squash; brush honey over chicken pieces. Roast 20 minutes or until chicken is cooked through (165°F). *Makes 4 to 6 servings*

Mustard-Grilled Red Snapper

½ cup Dijon mustard
1 tablespoon red wine vinegar
½ teaspoon black pepper
4 red snapper fillets (about 6 ounces each)

1. Spray grid with nonstick cooking spray. Prepare grill for direct cooking.

2. Combine mustard, vinegar and pepper in small bowl; mix well. Coat fish thoroughly with mustard mixture.

3. Grill fish over medium-high heat, covered, 8 minutes or until fish begins to flake when tested with fork, turning halfway through grilling time. *Makes 4 servings*

Sicilian-Style Pizza

2 loaves (1 pound each) frozen white bread dough
  Vegetable cooking spray
1¾ cups PREGO® Traditional Italian Sauce
2 cups shredded mozzarella cheese (about 8 ounces)

1. Thaw the bread dough according to the package directions. Heat the oven to 375°F. Spray a 15×10-inch jelly-roll pan with cooking spray. Place the dough loaves into the pan. Press the dough from the center out until it covers the bottom of the pan. Pinch the edges of the dough to form a rim.

2. Spread the sauce over the crust. Top with the cheese.

3. Bake for 25 minutes or until the cheese is melted and the crust is golden. *Makes 8 servings*

Kitchen Tip: To thaw the dough more quickly, place the dough into a microwavable dish. Brush with melted butter or spray with vegetable cooking spray. Microwave on LOW for 1 to 2 minutes.

Honey BBQ Bourbon Salmon

¾ cup *Cattlemen's*® Golden Honey Barbecue Sauce
3 tablespoons bourbon
4 salmon fillets, 4×2×1 inches
  Salt and black pepper to taste

1. Combine barbecue sauce and bourbon; set aside.

2. Season salmon with salt and pepper to taste. Generously spread barbecue sauce mixture on both sides of salmon fillets.

3. Cook salmon on well-greased grill over medium heat for 12 to 15 minutes until opaque in center, turning and basting once.* Serve with additional barbecue sauce. *Makes 4 servings*

*Alternate Cooking Directions—bake, broil or pan grill salmon as follows: Bake 10 to 15 minutes at 400°F. Broil 6 inches from heat about 10 minutes. Cook in a preheated, greased electric grill pan about 5 minutes.

Note: If desired, bourbon may be omitted or substituted with orange juice.

Prep Time: 5 minutes • **Cook Time:** 12 minutes

Chipotle Lamb Chops with Crispy Potatoes

4 lamb loin chops
2 teaspoons chipotle chili powder
   Salt and black pepper
8 ounces fingerling potatoes
2 tablespoons olive oil

1. Rub lamb chops with chili powder. Season with salt and pepper.

2. Cut potatoes into ¼-inch-thick slices. Heat oil in large nonstick skillet over medium heat. Add potatoes, stirring to coat with oil; season with salt and pepper. Cook 15 to 20 minutes or until golden brown and crispy, stirring occasionally.

3. Meanwhile, spray medium nonstick skillet with olive oil cooking spray. Add lamb chops; cook 12 to 15 minutes or until medium rare (145°F), turning once. Serve lamb chops with potatoes.

Makes 2 servings

Grilled Wasabi Flank Steak

6 tablespoons wasabi horseradish
2 tablespoons olive oil
1 beef flank steak (1 to 1½ pounds)
2 large red potatoes, cut into ¼-inch-thick slices
¼ cup water
1 teaspoon salt

1. Combine horseradish and oil in small bowl. Spread 2 tablespoons mixture on both sides of steak. Marinate in refrigerator 30 minutes or up to 2 hours.

2. Place potatoes, water and salt in microwavable dish; cover and microwave on HIGH 5 minutes. Drain potatoes. Add 2 tablespoons horseradish mixture; toss to coat.

3. Prepare grill for direct cooking. Grill steak over medium heat, covered, 8 minutes; turn. Place potatoes on grid. Brush potatoes and steak with remaining horseradish mixture. Grill 8 to 10 minutes or until steak is medium rare (145°F) and potatoes are slightly browned.

Makes 4 servings

Old-Fashioned Turkey Pot Pie

1 package (18 ounces) JENNIE-O TURKEY STORE® SO EASY
Turkey Breast Chunks In Homestyle Gravy
1½ cups frozen mixed vegetables, thawed
⅛ teaspoon black pepper
1 package (15 ounces) refrigerated pie crusts, divided

Preheat oven to 350°F.

In large bowl, combine turkey breast chunks in gravy, vegetables and pepper.

Press one pie crust in bottom and up side of 9-inch pie plate. Spoon turkey and vegetable mixture into crust. Place second crust over filling. Fold edges of crust inward and flute as desired to seal.

Bake 50 to 55 minutes or until crust is golden brown.

Cut into wedges and serve. *Makes 4 servings*

Open-Faced Steak and Blue Cheese Sandwiches

4 boneless beef top loin (strip) or tenderloin steaks,
cut ¾-inch thick
Black pepper
1 teaspoon olive oil
Salt
4 slices ciabatta bread
8 thin slices blue cheese

1. Season steaks with pepper. Heat oil in large nonstick skillet over medium heat.

2. Add steaks to skillet; do not crowd. Cook 10 to 12 minutes or until medium rare (145°F), turning once. Remove to cutting board. Tent with foil; let stand 5 to 10 minutes. Cut steaks into slices. Season with salt.

3. Toast bread. Place 2 slices blue cheese on each toast slice. Top cheese with steak slices. Serve immediately. *Makes 4 servings*

43

Crispy Onion Crescent Rolls

1 can (8 ounces) refrigerated crescent dinner rolls
1⅓ cups *French's*® French Fried Onions, slightly crushed
1 egg, beaten

1. Preheat oven to 375°F. Line large baking sheet with foil. Separate refrigerated rolls into 8 triangles. Sprinkle center of each triangle with about 1½ tablespoons French Fried Onions. Roll up triangles from short side, jelly-roll fashion. Sprinkle any excess onions over top of crescents.

2. Arrange crescents on prepared baking sheet. Brush with beaten egg. Bake 15 minutes or until golden brown and crispy. Transfer to wire rack; cool slightly. *Makes 8 servings*

Prep Time: 15 minutes • **Cook Time:** 15 minutes

Thai Curried Vegetables

1 can (about 13 ounces) coconut milk
1 tablespoon Thai red curry paste
1 bag (16 ounces) frozen Asian vegetable mixture, such as broccoli, carrots and water chestnuts
½ teaspoon salt

1. Combine coconut milk and curry paste in large saucepan. (Use less curry paste for a milder dish.) Cook and stir over medium-high heat 5 minutes.

2. Add vegetables; bring to a boil. Reduce heat to medium; cover and cook until vegetables are crisp-tender, stirring occasionally. *Makes 4 to 6 servings*

Bacon Roasted Brussels Sprouts

1 pound brussels sprouts
3 slices bacon, cut into ½-inch pieces
2 teaspoons brown sugar
Salt and black pepper

1. Preheat oven to 400°F. Trim ends from brussels sprouts; cut in half lengthwise.

2. Combine brussels sprouts, bacon and brown sugar in glass baking dish; mix well.

3. Roast 25 to 30 minutes or until golden brown, stirring halfway through cooking time. Season to taste with salt and pepper.

Makes 4 servings

Grilled Sweet Potatoes

4 medium-sized sweet potatoes (2 pounds), peeled
⅓ cup *French's*® Honey Dijon Mustard
2 tablespoons olive oil
1 tablespoon minced fresh rosemary *or* 1 teaspoon dried rosemary
½ teaspoon salt
¼ teaspoon black pepper

1. Cut potatoes diagonally into ½-inch-thick slices. Place potatoes and 1 cup water in shallow microwavable dish. Cover with vented plastic wrap and microwave on HIGH (100%) 6 minutes or until potatoes are crisp-tender, turning once. (Cook potatoes in two batches, if necessary.) Drain well.

2. Combine mustard, oil, rosemary, salt and pepper in small bowl; brush on potato slices. Place potatoes on oiled grid. Grill over medium-high heat 5 to 8 minutes or until potatoes are fork-tender, turning and basting often with mustard mixture.

Makes 4 servings

Tip: The task of selecting sweet potatoes is an easy one. Just look for medium-sized potatoes with thick, dark orange skins that are free from bruises. Sweet potatoes keep best in a dry, dark area at about 55°F. Under these conditions they should last about 3 to 4 weeks.

Pesto-Parmesan Twists

1 loaf (1 pound) frozen bread dough, thawed
¼ cup pesto
⅔ cup grated Parmesan cheese, divided
1 tablespoon olive oil

1. Line baking sheets with parchment paper. Roll out dough on lightly floured surface into 20×10-inch rectangle.

2. Spread pesto evenly over half of dough; sprinkle with ⅓ cup Parmesan. Fold remaining half of dough over filling, forming 10-inch square. Roll square into 12×10-inch rectangle. Cut into 12 (1-inch) strips with sharp knife. Cut strips in half crosswise to form 24 strips total.

3. Twist each strip several times; place on prepared baking sheets. Cover with plastic wrap; let rise in warm, draft-free place 20 minutes. Preheat oven to 350°F.

4. Brush breadsticks with oil; sprinkle with remaining ⅓ cup Parmesan. Bake 16 to 18 minutes or until golden brown.

Makes 24 breadsticks

Sautéed Snow Peas & Baby Carrots

1 tablespoon I CAN'T BELIEVE IT'S NOT BUTTER!® Spread
2 tablespoons chopped shallots or onion
5 ounces frozen whole baby carrots, partially thawed
4 ounces snow peas (about 1 cup)
2 teaspoons chopped fresh parsley (optional)

In 12-inch nonstick skillet, melt I Can't Believe It's Not Butter!® Spread over medium heat and cook shallots, stirring occasionally, 1 minute or until almost tender. Add carrots and snow peas and cook, stirring occasionally, 4 minutes or until crisp-tender. Stir in parsley, if desired, and heat through. *Makes 2 servings*

Note: Recipe can be doubled.

Apple Blossom Mold

1½ **cups boiling water**
  1 **package (8-serving size) or 2 packages (4-serving size each)**
    JELL-O® Brand Lemon Flavor Gelatin
  2 **cups cold apple juice**
  1 **cup diced red and green apples**

STIR boiling water into gelatin in large bowl at least 2 minutes until completely dissolved. Stir in cold juice. Refrigerate about 1½ hours or until thickened (spoon drawn through leaves definite impression). Stir in apples. Pour into 6-cup mold which has been sprayed with no stick cooking spray.

REFRIGERATE 4 hours or until firm. Unmold. Garnish as desired.

Makes 10 servings

Variation: Sugar Free Low Calorie Gelatin may be substituted.

Prep Time: 15 minutes • **Refrigerate Time:** 5½ hours

Broccoli with Garlic and Parmesan

  4 **cups fresh broccoli florets (about 12 ounces)**
  1 **tablespoon olive oil**
  3 **cloves garlic, thinly sliced**
  ¼ **cup water or reduced-sodium chicken broth**
  ¼ **cup grated Parmesan cheese**
    Salt and black pepper

1. Rinse broccoli; do not dry. Place in large microwavable bowl. Cover and microwave on HIGH 3 minutes or until crisp-tender.

2. Heat oil in large nonstick skillet over medium heat. Add garlic; cook and stir 2 minutes or until golden brown.

3. Add broccoli and water; cook and stir 2 minutes or until broccoli is tender and most of water is absorbed. Transfer to serving plate; top with Parmesan and season with salt and pepper.

Makes 4 servings

Cauliflower with Onion Butter

½ **cup (1 stick) butter, divided**
1 **cup diced onion**
1 **large head cauliflower, broken into florets**
½ **cup water**

1. Melt ¼ cup butter in medium skillet over medium heat. Add onion; cook and stir about 20 minutes or until onion is brown.

2. Meanwhile, place cauliflower and water in microwavable bowl. Microwave on HIGH 8 minutes or until crisp-tender; drain, if necessary.

3. Add remaining ¼ cup butter to skillet with onion; cook and stir until butter is melted. Pour over cooked cauliflower; serve immediately. *Makes about 8 servings*

Slow Cooker Cheddar Polenta

7 **cups hot water**
2 **cups polenta (not "quick-cooking") or coarse-ground yellow cornmeal**
2 **tablespoons extra-virgin olive oil**
2 **teaspoons salt**
3 **cups grated CABOT® Extra Sharp or Sharp Cheddar (about 12 ounces)**

Slow Cooker Directions

1. Combine water, polenta, olive oil and salt in slow cooker; whisk until well blended. Add cheese and whisk again.

2. Cover and cook on HIGH setting for 2 hours or until most liquid is absorbed. Stir well. (Polenta should have consistency of thick cooked cereal.) *Makes 8 servings*

Note: If not serving right away, pour onto oiled baking sheet with sides, spreading into even layer; cover with plastic wrap and let cool. When ready to serve, cut into rectangles and sauté in nonstick skillet with olive oil until golden on both sides.

Pullaparts

1 package (11 ounces) refrigerated French bread dough
1 tablespoon olive oil
½ teaspoon dried basil
2 tablespoons grated Parmesan cheese

1. Preheat oven to 350°F. Place dough on cutting board; cut into 12 slices with serrated knife.

2. Spray 9-inch round cake pan with butter-flavored cooking spray. Brush dough lightly with oil; arrange slices in pan, smooth side up, almost touching. Sprinkle with basil.

3. Bake 22 to 24 minutes or until rolls are golden and sound hollow when gently tapped. Remove to wire rack.

4. Lightly spray tops of rolls with cooking spray; sprinkle with Parmesan.   *Makes 12 rolls*

Glazed Acorn Squash

2 medium acorn squash, halved and seeded
1½ cups water
⅓ cup KARO® Light or Dark Corn Syrup
1 tablespoon margarine or butter, melted
½ teaspoon ground cinnamon
¼ teaspoon salt

1. Place squash cut side down in 13×9×2-inch baking dish; add water. Bake in 400°F oven 30 minutes or until squash is nearly fork-tender.

2. Turn squash cut side up. In small bowl, combine corn syrup, margarine, cinnamon and salt. Spoon corn syrup mixture into squash cavities.

3. Bake in 350°F oven 15 minutes or until fork-tender, basting occasionally.   *Makes 4 servings*

Prep Time: 5 minutes • **Bake Time:** 45 minutes

Rice Verde

3 cups cooked white rice
1 cup ORTEGA® Salsa Verde
4 ounces frozen spinach, thawed
½ teaspoon salt

Cook rice according to package directions; leave in saucepan.

Pour salsa into food processor. Add spinach. Pulse several times until spinach is thoroughly chopped and mixture is well combined.

Add salsa mixture and salt to saucepan with rice. Heat over medium heat, stirring until well mixed. Serve warm or at room temperature. *Makes 4 servings*

Prep Time: 5 minutes • **Start to Finish Time:** 15 minutes

Balsamic Green Beans with Almonds

1 pound fresh green beans, trimmed
1 tablespoon olive oil
2 teaspoons balsamic vinegar
½ teaspoon salt
¼ teaspoon black pepper
2 tablespoons sliced almonds, toasted*

*Toast almonds in a dry skillet over medium heat for 3 to 5 minutes or until fragrant, stirring frequently.

1. Place beans in medium saucepan; cover with water. Bring to a simmer over high heat. Reduce heat; simmer, uncovered, 4 to 8 minutes or until beans are crisp-tender. (Cooking time will vary depending on thickness of beans.) Drain well and return to saucepan.

2. Add oil, vinegar, salt and pepper; toss to coat. Sprinkle with almonds. *Makes 4 servings*

Roast Asparagus with Orange Butter

1 pound asparagus, trimmed
2 tablespoons butter, melted
2 tablespoons orange juice
½ teaspoon salt
¼ teaspoon black pepper
1½ teaspoons finely shredded or grated orange peel

1. Preheat oven to 425°F. Place asparagus in shallow 1½-quart baking dish. Combine melted butter and orange juice in small bowl; drizzle over asparagus. Sprinkle with salt and pepper; turn to coat.

2. Bake 12 minutes (for medium-sized asparagus) or until asparagus is crisp-tender. Sprinkle with orange peel.

Makes 4 servings

Diner Skillet Potatoes

3 pounds all-purpose potatoes, peeled and diced
2 large red or green bell peppers, chopped
1 envelope LIPTON® RECIPE SECRETS® Onion Soup Mix
2 tablespoons olive oil

1. In large bowl, combine potatoes, red peppers and soup mix until evenly coated.

2. In 12-inch nonstick skillet, heat oil over medium heat and cook potato mixture, covered, stirring occasionally, 12 minutes. Remove cover and continue cooking, stirring occasionally, 10 minutes or until potatoes are tender. *Makes about 6 servings*

Spicy Steak Fries

2 large potatoes
2 tablespoons MRS. DASH® Extra Spicy Seasoning Blend
2 tablespoons olive oil
1 clove garlic, minced

1. Wash and cut potatoes into wedges; do not peel. Dry potato slices on paper towels.

2. In a large bowl, toss potatoes with MRS. DASH® Extra Spicy Seasoning Blend, olive oil and garlic.

3. Spray baking sheet with nonstick cooking spray and lay wedges on baking sheet. Place potatoes in preheated 425°F oven and bake for 20 minutes. Turn the potatoes and bake another 15 minutes or until potatoes are browned and tender. *Makes 4 servings*

Prep Time: 10 minutes • **Cook Time:** 35 to 40 minutes

Skinny Mashed Sweet Potatoes

2 cans (14 ounces *each*) SWANSON® Chicken Broth (3½ cups)
4 large sweet potatoes *or* yams, peeled and cut into 1-inch
    pieces (about 7½ cups)
  Generous dash pepper
2 tablespoons packed brown sugar

1. In medium saucepan combine broth and potatoes. Over high heat, heat to a boil. Reduce heat to medium. Cover and cook 10 minutes or until potatoes are tender. Drain, reserving broth.

2. Mash potatoes with **1¼ cups** broth and pepper. If needed, add additional broth until potatoes are desired consistency. Add brown sugar. *Makes about 6 servings*

Prep Time: 10 minutes • **Cook Time:** 15 minutes

Crème Brûlée

2 cups whipping cream
4 egg yolks
¼ cup plus 2 tablespoons sugar, divided

1. Preheat oven to 300°F. Heat cream in heavy medium saucepan over medium-low heat until small bubbles appear around edge of pan (130° to 140°F).

2. Whisk egg yolks and ¼ cup sugar in medium bowl until well blended. Slowly whisk in cream until blended. Pour mixture into 6 small shallow baking dishes or 4-ounce custard cups. Place dishes in 13×9-inch baking pan. Fill pan with hot water until water reaches halfway up sides of dishes.

3. Bake 25 to 30 minutes for shallow dishes and 30 to 35 minutes for custard cups or until set in center. (Mixture may look thin but will set upon cooling.) Cool to room temperature. Refrigerate at least 4 hours or up to 24 hours.

4. Preheat broiler. Sprinkle remaining 2 tablespoons sugar evenly over custards. Broil 6 inches from heat, rotating if necessary to brown sugar evenly, about 30 seconds or until golden crust forms. Serve immediately. *Makes 6 servings*

Tip: For extra flavor, add 1 teaspoon vanilla to cream mixture in step 2.

Tiramisu

1 container (8 ounces) mascarpone cheese
12 ounces prepared cappuccino drink, divided
2 packages (3 ounces each) ladyfingers

1. Whisk mascarpone and ¼ cup cappuccino drink in medium bowl 2 minutes or until thickened.

2. Dip ladyfingers in remaining cappuccino drink. Tightly arrange 1 package ladyfingers to cover bottom of 6-inch square dish.

3. Spread half of mascarpone mixture over ladyfingers. Repeat layers with remaining ladyfingers and mascarpone mixture.

Makes 4 to 6 servings

Tip: Sprinkle the tiramisu with cocoa powder or grated chocolate.

Frozen Chocolate-Covered Bananas

2 ripe medium bananas
4 wooden craft sticks
½ cup granola cereal without raisins
⅓ cup hot fudge topping, at room temperature

1. Line baking sheet with waxed paper.

2. Peel bananas; cut each in half crosswise. Insert wooden stick into center of cut end of each banana about 1½ inches into banana half. Place on prepared baking sheet; freeze 2 hours or until firm.

3. Place granola in large resealable food storage bag; crush slightly using rolling pin or meat mallet. Transfer granola to shallow plate. Place hot fudge topping in shallow dish.

4. Working with 1 banana at a time, place frozen banana in hot fudge topping; turn and spread topping evenly over banana with spatula. Immediately place banana on plate with granola; turn to coat. Return to baking sheet. Repeat with remaining bananas.

5. Freeze at least 2 hours or until hot fudge topping is very firm. Let stand 5 minutes before serving.

Makes 4 servings

Chocolate Cherry Turnovers

1 package (8 ounces) refrigerated crescent roll dough
¾ cup semisweet chocolate chips, divided
½ cup canned cherry pie filling

1. Preheat oven to 375°F. Line baking sheet with parchment paper.

2. Unroll dough onto clean work surface; separate into 4 rectangles. Press perforations firmly to seal. Cut off corners of rectangles with sharp paring knife to form oval shapes.

3. Place 1 tablespoon chocolate chips on half of each oval; top with 2 tablespoons pie filling. Sprinkle with additional 1 tablespoon chocolate chips. Fold dough over filling; press edges to seal. Crimp edges with fork, if desired. Place turnovers on prepared baking sheet.

4. Bake 14 minutes or until golden brown. Cool on baking sheet 5 minutes. Melt remaining chocolate chips; drizzle over turnovers. Serve warm. *Makes 4 turnovers*

Caramelized Pineapple

1 tablespoon butter
2 cups fresh pineapple chunks
3 tablespoons sugar
2 cups vanilla ice cream or frozen yogurt

1. Spray baking sheet with nonstick cooking spray.

2. Heat butter in large nonstick skillet over medium-high heat. Combine pineapple and sugar in skillet; cook and stir about 7 minutes or until pineapple begins to brown. Cook 2 to 4 minutes more or until golden brown, stirring occasionally. Spread on prepared baking sheet; cool 5 minutes.

3. Spoon pineapple into 4 dessert dishes; top with ice cream. Serve immediately. *Makes 4 servings*

Coconut Cream Pie

1½ cups sweetened shredded coconut
8 snack-size containers prepared vanilla pudding
1 (6-ounce) graham cracker pie crust

1. Preheat oven to 350°F. Spread coconut on baking sheet. Toast coconut 10 minutes, stirring frequently; cool. Reserve 2 tablespoons coconut.

2. Combine pudding and remaining coconut in medium bowl.

3. Pour pudding mixture into pie crust; sprinkle with reserved coconut. Refrigerate 1 to 2 hours or until pudding is set.

Makes 8 servings

Milano® Cookie Caramel Ice Cream Cake

1 package (6 ounces) PEPPERIDGE FARM® Milano Cookies
3 cups vanilla or chocolate ice cream, softened
⅓ cup prepared caramel topping

1. Line an 8-inch round cake pan with plastic wrap.

2. Cut the cookies in half crosswise and arrange around the edge of the pan. Place the remaining cookies in the bottom of the pan.

3. Spread **1½ cups** ice cream over the cookies. Drizzle with the caramel topping. Spread the remaining ice cream over the caramel topping. Cover and freeze for 6 hours or until the ice cream is firm.

4. Uncover the pan and invert the cake onto a serving plate. Serve with additional caramel topping.   *Makes 8 servings*

Kitchen Tip: Substitute chocolate topping for caramel topping.

Prep Time: 20 minutes • **Freeze Time:** 6 hours

Blueberry Muffin Bread Pudding

1 tablespoon butter, melted
1½ cups milk
2 eggs
4 packages (2 ounces each) mini blueberry muffins, cut into 1-inch pieces

1. Preheat oven to 350°F. Brush 4 (6-ounce) ramekins or custard cups with melted butter.

2. Whisk milk and eggs in medium bowl until well blended. Add muffins; toss to coat. Let stand 15 minutes to allow muffins to absorb milk mixture.

3. Spoon mixture into prepared ramekins. Bake 15 minutes or until lightly browned. *Makes 4 servings*

Serving Suggestion: Serve with a dollop of whipped cream and fresh blueberries.

Raspberry Mousse

1 container (10 ounces) frozen raspberries in syrup
1 package (4-serving size) raspberry-flavored gelatin
¼ cup water
2 cups whipping cream

1. Process raspberries with syrup in food processor or blender until smooth. Press through fine mesh sieve to remove seeds. Set aside.

2. Heat gelatin and water in small saucepan over medium heat 5 to 7 minutes or until mixture is very syrupy, stirring occasionally. Remove from heat. Cool slightly.

3. Beat cream in large bowl with electric mixer at high speed 3 to 5 minutes or until soft peaks form. Add raspberries and gelatin mixture; beat 3 to 5 minutes or until well blended.

4. Pour into individual serving dishes; refrigerate 2 hours or until set. *Makes 4 to 6 servings*

Mini Pain au Chocolate

½ **cup sugar, divided**
1 **package (15 ounces) refrigerated pie crusts (2 crusts)**
1 **cup semisweet chocolate chips**

1. Preheat oven to 400°F. Spray baking sheet with nonstick cooking spray or line with parchment paper.

2. Sprinkle 2 tablespoons sugar on cutting board or work surface. Unroll 1 pie crust over sugar. Sprinkle crust with 2 tablespoons sugar. Using pizza wheel or sharp knife, trim away 1 inch dough from four sides to form square. (Save dough trimmings for another use or discard.)

3. Cut square in half; cut each half crosswise into 4 pieces to form 8 small (4×2-inch) rectangles. Place heaping teaspoon chocolate chips at one short end of each rectangle; roll up. Place rolls, seam side down, on prepared baking sheet. Repeat with remaining sugar, pie crust and chocolate chips.

4. Bake 12 to 14 minutes or until lightly browned. Cool 10 minutes to serve warm, or cool completely. *Makes 16 rolls*

Vanilla Rice Pudding

3 **cups milk, divided**
1 **cup MINUTE® White Rice, uncooked**
⅓ **cup raisins (optional)**
1 **package (4-serving size) vanilla-flavor instant pudding and pie filling**

Bring 1 cup milk to a boil in medium saucepan. Stir in rice and raisins, if desired; cover. Remove from heat. Let stand 5 minutes.

Prepare pudding as directed on package in large bowl with remaining 2 cups milk.

Add rice mixture to prepared pudding; mix well. Cover surface of pudding with plastic wrap; cool 5 minutes. Serve warm or chilled.
Makes 6 servings

Variation: Serve sprinkled with ground cinnamon or 1 cup shredded coconut.

Strawberry Napoleons

1 quart fresh strawberries
1 sheet frozen puff pastry (half of 17¼-ounce package), thawed
1 container (8 ounces) whipped topping

1. Remove stems from strawberries. Slice strawberries into large bowl; set aside until ready to use.

2. Preheat oven to 400°F. Line baking sheet with parchment paper. Unfold pastry sheet; cut into 3 strips along fold marks. Cut each strip crosswise into thirds to form 9 squares total. Place pastry squares on prepared baking sheet. Bake 12 to 15 minutes or until puffed and golden brown. Remove to wire rack to cool completely.

3. For each napoleon, split 1 puff pastry square in half horizontally. Place 1 half on serving plate; top with whipped topping and strawberries. Repeat layers.   *Makes 9 napoleons*

Sweet Fruit Dip

4 ounces (½ of 8-ounce package) PHILADELPHIA®
**   Cream Cheese, softened**
1 cup whole berry cranberry sauce
1 cup thawed COOL WHIP® Whipped Topping

BEAT cream cheese and cranberry sauce with electric mixer on medium speed until well blended. Gently stir in whipped topping; cover.

REFRIGERATE at least 1 hour or until ready to serve.

SERVE with strawberries, red and green grapes, pineapple, kiwi or pears, cut into bite-size pieces for dipping.
                    Makes 16 servings (2 tablespoons each)

Substitution: Prepare as directed, using PHILADELPHIA® Neufchâtel Cheese, ⅓ Less Fat than Cream Cheese and COOL WHIP® LITE® Whipped Topping.

Prep Time: 10 minutes • **Total Time:** 1 hour 10 minutes

Mango Cheesecake

1 package (16 ounces) frozen mango chunks
1 package (24 ounces) ready-to-eat cheesecake filling
1 (6-ounce) graham cracker pie crust

1. Thaw mango at room temperature about 20 minutes to soften slightly. Reserve some pieces for garnish, if desired. Place remaining mango in food processor; process with on/off pulses until finely chopped. *Do not purée.*

2. Transfer mango to large bowl; stir in cheesecake filling until blended. Fill pie crust with mango mixture (about 1 cup mixture will be left over); smooth top.

3. Cover and freeze until ready to serve. Let stand at room temperature 10 minutes before serving.   *Makes 8 servings*

Quick Peach Crisp

4 cups sliced peeled peaches or nectarines (about 4 large peaches or nectarines)
3 tablespoons cinnamon-sugar
12 to 14 pecan shortbread cookies,* coarsely chopped

*Twenty coarsely chopped vanilla wafers can be substituted for the shortbread.

1. Preheat oven to 350°F. Place peaches in 9-inch square baking dish. Add cinnamon-sugar; toss gently until well mixed. Top with cookies.

2. Bake 25 to 30 minutes or until peaches are cooked through and cookies are lightly browned.   *Makes 5 servings*

Tip: Cinnamon-sugar is available in most large supermarkets in the spice or baking section. Or you can easily make your own by mixing 1 cup sugar and 1 tablespoon ground cinnamon. Store cinnamon-sugar in a glass jar.

Strawberry Crêpes

1 cup whipping cream
1 package (16 ounces) frozen sweetened sliced strawberries, thawed, divided
1 package (5 ounces) crêpes (10 crêpes)

1. Beat cream in large chilled bowl with electric mixer at high speed until stiff peaks form.

2. Chop half of strawberries; stir into whipped cream. Spoon about 2 tablespoons mixture down center of each crêpe; roll up. Cover and refrigerate until ready to serve.

3. Process remaining strawberries in food processor until smooth. Drizzle over crêpes. *Makes 8 to 10 crêpes*

Dark Chocolate Mousse

4 squares BAKER'S SELECT® Bittersweet Chocolate
1 tub (8 ounces) COOL WHIP® Whipped Topping, thawed
½ cup fresh raspberries

MICROWAVE chocolate in microwavable bowl on HIGH 1½ minutes, stirring with whisk every 45 seconds until melted.

ADD 1 cup COOL WHIP®; stir until blended. Stir in remaining COOL WHIP®.

SPOON into dessert dishes; top with raspberries.
Makes 6 servings (about ½ cup each)

Substitution: Prepare as directed, using BAKER'S® Semi-Sweet Chocolate.

Prep Time: 10 minutes

Upside-Down Apple Tart

1 sheet frozen puff pastry (half of 17¼-ounce package), thawed
1½ tablespoons butter, softened
½ cup packed brown sugar
5 to 6 large apples (about 3½ pounds)

1. Unfold pastry sheet on cutting board; trim into 8-inch circle. Place pastry circle on baking sheet and refrigerate until needed. Preheat oven to 375°F.

2. Grease side and bottom of 8-inch cast iron skillet with butter (use entire amount). Spread sugar evenly over bottom of skillet. Peel apples; cut into quarters. Remove cores and cut into thick wedges. Arrange apple wedges vertically in prepared skillet in tight concentric circles. Wedges should extend over top of skillet by about 1 inch. (Apples will shrink as they cook.)

3. Place skillet over medium heat and cook, undisturbed, 15 minutes or until sugar bubbles up. Place skillet in oven on large sheet of foil to catch drips. Bake 15 to 20 minutes or until apples begin to shrink.

4. Carefully remove tart from oven and fit pastry circle over top of skillet. (Skillet and apples will be very hot.) Tuck excess dough around edge using butter knife. Return skillet to oven; bake 15 to 20 minutes or until pastry is puffed and browned.

5. Remove skillet to wire rack; cool at least 15 minutes. Place serving plate over top of skillet. Using oven mitts, invert skillet and shake tart onto plate to release.   *Makes 6 servings*

Tips: Sprinkle cinnamon over the apples before cooking. Serve the tart warm with whipped cream or ice cream.

∞ ∞ ∞

When using only one sheet of puff pasty,
wrap the remaining sheet of pastry in
plastic wrap or foil and return it to
the freezer as soon as possible.

4 Ingredient
cookbook

Contents

Starters & Snacks

Chili Puffs

1 package (17¼ ounces) frozen puff pastry, thawed
1 can (about 15 ounces) chili without beans
½ (8-ounce) package cream cheese, softened
½ cup (2 ounces) finely shredded sharp Cheddar cheese
   Sliced green onions (optional)

1. Preheat oven to 400°F.

2. Roll each pastry sheet on lightly floured surface into 18×9-inch rectangle. Cut each rectangle into 18 (3-inch) squares. Press pastry into 36 mini (1¾-inch) muffin cups. Bake 10 minutes.

3. Combine chili and cream cheese in medium bowl until smooth. Fill each pastry shell with 2 teaspoons chili mixture, pressing down centers of pastry to fill, if necessary. Sprinkle evenly with Cheddar.

4. Bake 5 to 7 minutes or until Cheddar is melted and edges of pastry are golden brown. Let stand in pans 5 minutes. Garnish with green onions. *Makes 36 puffs*

Tip: Use a pizza cutter to easily cut puff pastry sheets.

◎◎◎

For the best results, thaw puff pastry in the
refrigerator. A whole package will take
about 6 hours to thaw and can be kept
in the refrigerator for up to two days.

Grilled Margarita Shrimp

1 cup margarita mix
1 cup ORTEGA® Taco Sauce, divided
2 pounds raw shrimp (21 to 30 count), peeled and deveined
3 tablespoons ORTEGA® Diced Green Chiles

Combine margarita mix, ½ cup taco sauce and shrimp in large bowl; toss well. Marinate in refrigerator 30 minutes or up to 2 hours.

Preheat grill until piping hot, about 15 minutes. Grill shrimp 4 minutes on each side or until shrimp turn pink.

Combine remaining ½ cup taco sauce and chiles. Use as dipping sauce for shrimp.   *Makes 6 servings*

Prep Time: 40 minutes • **Start to Finish Time:** 50 minutes

Pepperoni-Oregano Focaccia

1 tablespoon cornmeal
1 package (about 13 ounces) refrigerated pizza dough
½ cup finely chopped pepperoni (3 to 3½ ounces)
1½ teaspoons finely chopped fresh oregano *or* ½ teaspoon dried oregano
1 tablespoon olive oil

1. Preheat oven to 425°F. Spray baking sheet with nonstick cooking spray; sprinkle with cornmeal.

2. Unroll dough onto lightly floured surface. Pat dough into 12×9-inch rectangle. Sprinkle half of pepperoni and half of oregano over one side of dough. Fold over dough to form 12×4½-inch rectangle.

3. Roll dough into 12×9-inch rectangle. Place on prepared baking sheet. Prick dough with fork at 2-inch intervals (about 30 times). Brush with oil; sprinkle with remaining pepperoni and oregano.

4. Bake 12 to 15 minutes or until golden brown. (Prick dough several more times if dough puffs as it bakes.) Cut into strips.

Makes 12 servings

85

Blue Cheese Mushrooms

1 pound medium fresh mushrooms
¼ cup sliced green onions
1 tablespoon butter or margarine
1 package (4 ounces) ATHENOS® Crumbled Blue Cheese
3 ounces PHILADELPHIA® Cream Cheese, softened

PREHEAT broiler. Remove stems from mushrooms; chop stems. Cook and stir stems and onions in butter in small skillet on medium heat until tender.

ADD blue cheese and cream cheese; mix well. Spoon evenly into mushroom caps; place on rack of broiler pan.

BROIL 2 to 3 minutes or until golden brown. Serve warm.
Makes about 2 dozen or 24 servings (1 mushroom each)

Prep Time: 30 minutes • **Broil Time:** 3 minutes

Warm French Onion Dip with Crusty Bread

1 can (10½ ounces) CAMPBELL'S® Condensed French Onion Soup
1 package (8 ounces) cream cheese, softened
1 cup shredded mozzarella cheese
Crusty bread cubes, crackers or vegetables

1. Heat the oven to 375°F. Stir the soup and cream cheese in a medium bowl until it's smooth. Stir in the mozzarella cheese. Spread in a 1½-quart shallow baking dish.

2. Bake for 30 minutes or until the mixture is hot and bubbling.

3. Serve with the bread for dipping. *Makes 2 cups*

Kitchen Tip: To soften the cream cheese, remove it from the wrapper. On a microwavable plate, microwave on HIGH for 15 seconds.

Prep Time: 15 minutes • **Bake Time:** 30 minutes

Turkey Canapés

**8 slices JENNIE-O TURKEY STORE® Turkey Pastrami, Turkey Salami
  or Turkey Ham**
32 buttery round crackers, wheat crackers or rye crackers
**¾ cup (6 ounces) cream cheese with chives or herb-flavored
  cream cheese**
1 small cucumber
Fresh dill (optional)

Cut each slice of turkey into quarters; set aside. Spread each
cracker with about 1 teaspoon cream cheese. Fold turkey
quarters in half. Place turkey on cream cheese. Cut cucumber
lengthwise in half; cut each half into ¼-inch slices. Top each
cracker with cucumber slice and garnish with fresh dill, if desired.

Makes 32 servings

Prep Time: 30 minutes

Spicy Roasted Chickpeas

1 can (about 19 ounces) chickpeas, rinsed and drained
2 tablespoons olive oil
½ teaspoon salt
½ teaspoon black pepper
¾ to 1 tablespoon chili powder
⅛ to ¼ teaspoon ground red pepper
1 lime, cut into wedges

1. Preheat oven to 400°F.

2. Combine chickpeas, oil, salt and black pepper in large
bowl. Spread in single layer on 15×10-inch jelly-roll pan. Roast
15 minutes or until chickpeas begin to brown, shaking pan twice.

3. Sprinkle with chili powder and red pepper to taste; roast
5 minutes or until dark golden-red. Serve with lime wedges.

Makes 4 servings

Asparagus & Prosciutto Antipasto

12 asparagus spears (about 8 ounces)
2 ounces cream cheese, softened
¼ cup (1 ounce) crumbled blue cheese or goat cheese
¼ teaspoon black pepper
1 package (3 to 4 ounces) thinly sliced prosciutto

1. Trim and discard tough ends of asparagus spears. Simmer asparagus in salted water in large skillet 4 to 5 minutes or until crisp-tender. Drain; rinse with cold water until cool. Drain; pat dry with paper towels.

2. Combine cream cheese, blue cheese and pepper in small bowl; mix well. Cut prosciutto slices in half crosswise to make 12 pieces. Spread cream cheese mixture evenly over one side of each prosciutto slice.

3. Wrap each asparagus spear with prosciutto slice. Serve at room temperature or slightly chilled. *Makes 12 appetizers*

Shrimp Picadas

24 small shrimp, shelled and deveined (about 1 pound)
1 bottle (8 ounces) ORTEGA® Enchilada Sauce
12 (8-inch) ORTEGA® Soft Flour Tortillas
1 cup (4 ounces) shredded pepper jack cheese

Preheat oven to 350°F. Lightly coat 24 mini (1¾-inch) muffin cups with nonstick cooking spray; set aside.

Combine shrimp and enchilada sauce in skillet over medium-low heat. Cook and stir 5 minutes or until shrimp are cooked and sauce is reduced.

Cut rounds from tortillas with 2-inch cookie cutter. Press rounds into prepared muffin cups. Place one cooked shrimp into each tortilla cup. Evenly top with sauce; sprinkle with cheese.

Bake 12 to 15 minutes or until cheese is melted and tortilla cups are browned. *Makes 24 appetizers*

Tip: For a heartier serving, use a regular-size muffin pan. Prepare the picadas using a larger cookie cutter, and divide the ingredients equally among the muffin cups as directed.

Tomato Pesto Tart

PAM® Original No-Stick Cooking Spray
1 frozen puff pastry sheet, thawed according to package
directions (1 sheet = half of 17.3-ounce package)
½ cup prepared basil pesto
1 cup shredded part-skim mozzarella cheese (4 ounces)
1 can (14.5 ounces) HUNT'S® Whole Peeled Tomatoes, drained,
cut into ¼-inch-thick slices
Thinly sliced fresh basil (optional)

Preheat oven to 400°F. Spray rimmed baking sheet with cooking spray; set aside. Unfold 1 puff pastry sheet onto lightly floured surface; roll out to 12-inch square. Crimp edges; place on prepared baking sheet.

Spread pesto evenly over puff pastry. Sprinkle with ½ cup cheese, then add tomato slices in a single layer. Finish by topping evenly with remaining cheese.

Bake 17 to 20 minutes or until golden brown. Garnish with fresh basil, if desired. For small bites, cut into 16 pieces. Serve immediately. *Makes 9 servings (1 piece each)*

Cook's Tips: Garnishing with fresh basil adds another layer of taste plus taste-tempting aromatics. Wow guests with this simple yet upscale "small bite" appetizer. For variation, you may use HUNT'S® Diced Tomatoes with Balsamic Vinegar, Basil & Olive Oil in place of whole tomatoes. Or, HUNT'S® Petite Diced Tomatoes may be used—they require no slicing or dicing!

Hands On Time: 10 minutes • **Total Time:** 30 minutes

◎◎◎
Great prepared pesto is easy to find in
your grocer's refrigerated section.

Hot 'n' Honeyed Chicken Wings

1 cup PACE® Picante Sauce
¼ cup honey
½ teaspoon ground ginger
12 chicken wings or chicken drummettes

1. Stir the picante sauce, honey and ginger in a small bowl.

2. Cut the chicken wings at the joints into 24 pieces. Discard the tips or save them for another use. Put the wings in a small bowl. Add the picante sauce mixture and toss to coat. Put the wings on a foil-lined shallow baking pan.

3. Bake at 400°F for 55 minutes or until the wings are glazed and cooked through,* turning and brushing often with sauce during the last 30 minutes of cooking.   *Makes 24 appetizers*

*The internal temperature of the chicken should reach 170°F.

Prep Time: 10 minutes • **Bake Time:** 55 minutes

Olive Twists

1 package (11 ounces) refrigerated breadstick dough
    (12 breadsticks)
1 egg white, beaten
12 pimiento-stuffed green olives, chopped
¼ teaspoon paprika

1. Preheat oven to 375°F. Line baking sheet with parchment paper.

2. Separate breadstick dough into individual sticks. Brush dough lightly with egg white; sprinkle with olives and paprika. Twist each stick 3 or 4 times.

3. Bake 11 to 13 minutes or until golden. Serve warm.
                    Makes 12 servings

Chipotle-Spiced Nuts

1 pound mixed nuts
4 tablespoons butter, melted
2 tablespoons ORTEGA® Chipotle Taco Seasoning Mix
1 tablespoon light brown sugar

Preheat oven to 325°F. Toss nuts, butter, seasoning mix and brown sugar in large bowl until well combined.

Spread nut mixture on baking pan. Bake 20 minutes, stirring after 10 minutes. Serve warm, if desired. To store, allow to cool, and place in airtight container for up to 2 weeks.   *Makes 1 pound*

Tip: Try sprinkling these nuts over your favorite ice cream for a flavorful "hot" and cold dessert.

Prep Time: 5 minutes • **Start to Finish Time:** 25 minutes

Baked Cream Cheese Appetizer

1 can (4 ounces) refrigerated crescent dinner rolls
1 package (8 ounces) PHILADELPHIA® Cream Cheese
½ teaspoon dill weed
1 egg white, beaten

UNROLL dough on lightly greased cookie sheet; firmly press perforations together to form 12×4-inch rectangle.

SPRINKLE cream cheese with dill; lightly press dill into cream cheese. Place cream cheese, dill-side up, in center of dough. Bring edges of dough up over cream cheese; press edges of dough together to seal, completely enclosing cream cheese. Brush with egg white.

BAKE at 350°F for 15 to 18 minutes or until lightly browned. Serve with NABISCO® Crackers, French bread or fresh fruit slices.
Makes 8 servings

Great Substitutes: Substitute ½ teaspoon dried rosemary leaves, crushed, combined with ½ teaspoon paprika for the dill weed.

Prep Time: 10 minutes • **Bake Time:** 18 minutes

Croque Monsieur Bites

8 thin slices firm sandwich bread
4 slices Swiss cheese, halved (about 4 ounces)
4 slices smoked ham (about 4 ounces)
  Dash grated nutmeg
2 tablespoons butter, melted

1. Cut crusts from bread. Place 4 slices bread on work surface. Layer each with half slice cheese, ham slice and another half slice cheese; sprinkle with nutmeg. Top with remaining 4 slices bread. Brush outside of sandwiches with melted butter.

2. Cook sandwiches in large skillet over medium heat 2 to 3 minutes per side or until golden brown and cheese is melted. Cut into quarters. *Makes 16 pieces*

Tip: These sandwiches can be prepared ahead of time and reheated for an easy party appetizer. Leave sandwiches whole after cooking and refrigerate until ready to serve. Cut into quarters and place on foil-lined baking sheet. Bake in preheated 350°F oven about 8 minutes or until sandwiches are heated through and cheese is melted.

Pepperoni Pizza Dip

1 cup RAGÚ® Old World Style® Pasta Sauce
1 cup RAGÚ® Cheesy! Classic Alfredo Sauce
1 cup shredded mozzarella cheese (about 4 ounces)
¼ to ½ cup finely chopped pepperoni

1. In 2-quart saucepan, heat Pasta Sauces, cheese and pepperoni, stirring occasionally, 10 minutes or until cheese is melted.

2. Pour into 1½-quart casserole or serving dish and serve, if desired, with breadsticks, sliced Italian bread or crackers. *Makes 2 cups dip*

Prep Time: 5 minutes • **Cook Time:** 10 minutes

Quick-Fix Dinners

Barbecued Pork Spareribs

4 pounds pork spareribs, cut into serving-sized pieces
1 can (10¼ ounces) CAMPBELL'S® Beef Gravy
¾ cup barbecue sauce
2 tablespoons packed brown sugar

1. Place the ribs into an 8-quart saucepot. Pour water into the saucepot to cover. Heat over high heat to a boil. Reduce the heat to low. Cover and cook for 30 minutes or until the ribs are tender. Drain.

2. Stir the gravy, barbecue sauce and brown sugar in a large bowl. Add the ribs and toss to coat.

3. Lightly oil the grill rack and heat the grill to medium-high. Grill the ribs for 10 minutes or until they're cooked through, turning and brushing occasionally with the gravy mixture.

Makes 4 servings

Prep Time: 15 minutes • **Cook Time:** 30 minutes • **Grill Time:** 10 minutes

◎◎◎
Use the gravy mixture as a basting
sauce when grilling chicken.

Chicken with Bacon-Tomato Sauce

  2 cups fire-roasted diced tomatoes*
  4 pounds bone-in chicken pieces (about 8 pieces)
  ¾ teaspoon salt, divided
  ¼ teaspoon black pepper
  6 slices bacon, cut into 1-inch pieces
  1 onion, cut into ½-inch pieces

*Fire-roasted tomatoes give this dish a deeper, more complex flavor. They can be found in the supermarket with other canned tomato products.

1. Preheat oven to 450°F. Spread tomatoes on bottom of 13×9-inch baking dish.

2. Season chicken with ½ teaspoon salt and pepper. Spray large nonstick skillet with nonstick cooking spray; heat over medium-high heat. Add chicken; cook 8 minutes or until browned and crisp, turning once.

3. Transfer to prepared baking dish. Bake 30 to 40 minutes or until chicken is cooked through (165°F).

4. Meanwhile, cook bacon in medium skillet over medium-high heat 8 minutes or until crisp, stirring occasionally. Transfer to paper towels to drain. Cook onion in drippings 8 minutes or until golden, stirring occasionally. Drain fat. Stir in remaining ¼ teaspoon salt.

5. Transfer chicken and tomatoes to serving plate; top with bacon and onion.   *Makes 4 servings*

Asian Grilled Steak

¾ cup WISH-BONE® Italian Dressing*
 3 tablespoons soy sauce
 3 tablespoons firmly packed brown sugar
 ½ teaspoon ground ginger (optional)
 1 (1- to 1½-pound) flank, top round or sirloin steak

Also terrific with WISH-BONE® Robusto Italian, Light Italian or Red Wine Vinaigrette Dressing.

Combine all ingredients except steak in small bowl. Pour ½ cup marinade over steak in large, shallow nonaluminum baking dish or resealable plastic bag. Cover, or close bag, and marinate in refrigerator, turning occasionally, 30 minutes or up to 24 hours. Refrigerate remaining marinade.

Remove steak from marinade, discarding marinade. Grill or broil steak, turning once and brushing frequently with reserved marinade, until steak reaches desired doneness. Let stand 10 minutes; thinly slice and serve.   *Makes 4 servings*

Prep Time: 5 minutes • **Marinate Time:** 3 hours •
Cook Time: 15 minutes

Baked Manicotti

1 jar (1 pound 10 ounces) RAGÚ® Old World Style® Pasta Sauce
 8 fresh or frozen prepared manicotti
 ½ cup (about 2 ounces) shredded mozzarella cheese
 2 tablespoons grated Parmesan cheese

1. Preheat oven to 450°F.

2. In 13×9-inch baking dish, spread half of the Pasta Sauce; arrange manicotti over sauce. Top with remaining sauce. Sprinkle with cheeses.

3. Bake, covered, 20 minutes. Remove cover and continue baking 5 minutes or until heated through.   *Makes 4 servings*

Chicken & Mushrooms with Pasta & Roasted Garlic Sauce

1 tablespoon olive oil
4 boneless skinless chicken breasts
1 jar (about 28 ounces) roasted garlic pasta sauce
1 cup sliced mushrooms
8 ounces rotini or fusilli pasta, cooked and drained
Grated Parmesan cheese (optional)

1. Heat oil in large skillet over medium heat. Brown chicken. Remove from skillet; cut into thin strips. Return to skillet.

2. Stir in pasta sauce and mushrooms. Cover and simmer 10 minutes or until chicken is cooked through. Stir in pasta. Sprinkle with Parmesan, if desired.   *Makes 4 servings*

Tilapia with Spinach and Feta

1 teaspoon olive oil
1 clove garlic, minced
4 cups baby spinach
2 skinless fillets tilapia or other mild, medium-textured white fish
   (4 ounces each)
¼ teaspoon black pepper
2 ounces feta cheese, cut into 2 (3-inch) pieces

1. Preheat oven to 350°F. Spray baking sheet with nonstick cooking spray.

2. Heat oil in medium skillet over medium-low heat. Add garlic; cook and stir 2 minutes. Add spinach; cook, stirring occasionally, just until wilted.

3. Arrange fillets on prepared baking sheet; sprinkle with pepper. Place one piece of feta on each fillet; top with spinach mixture.

4. Fold one end of each fillet up and over spinach filling; secure with toothpick. Repeat with opposite end of each fillet.

5. Bake about 20 minutes or until fish begins to flake when tested with fork.   *Makes 2 servings*

Chunky Beef Chili

1½ pounds beef for stew, cut into 1- to 1½-inch pieces
2 tablespoons oil, divided
Salt
1 medium onion, chopped
1 jalapeño pepper, minced
2 cans (about 14 ounces each) chili-seasoned diced tomatoes

1. Heat 1 tablespoon oil in Dutch oven over medium heat until hot. Brown half of beef; remove from Dutch oven. Repeat with remaining beef. Remove beef from Dutch oven. Season with salt, as desired.

2. Add remaining 1 tablespoon oil, onion and jalapeño pepper to Dutch oven. Cook and stir 5 to 8 minutes or until vegetables are tender. Return beef and juices to Dutch oven. Add tomatoes; bring to a boil. Reduce heat; cover tightly and simmer 1¾ to 2¼ hours or until beef is fork-tender. *Makes 4 servings*

Tip: Canned Mexican or Southwest-style diced tomatoes may be substituted for chili-seasoned tomatoes.

Prep and Cook Time: 2 to 2¾ hours
*Favorite recipe from **Courtesy The Beef Checkoff***

Baked Oriental Chicken

6 boneless skinless chicken breast halves (4 ounces each)
⅔ cup oriental plum sauce
1 tablespoon MRS. DASH® Extra Spicy Seasoning Blend
1 tablespoon lite soy sauce

1. Preheat oven to 375°F. Place chicken in a nonstick baking pan.

2. Combine plum sauce, MRS. DASH® Extra Spicy Seasoning Blend and soy sauce in small bowl. Pour mixture evenly over chicken, turning pieces until well coated.

3. Bake uncovered 35 to 40 minutes or until chicken reaches 170°F. *Makes 6 servings*

Prep Time: 10 minutes • **Cook Time:** 35 to 40 minutes

Prune-Stuffed Pork Loin Roast

1 (2½-pound) boneless pork loin or sirloin roast, well trimmed
9 large pitted dried plums*
2 tablespoons apricot preserves
2 teaspoons Dijon mustard
 Black pepper

*Dried plums should be moist. If not, soak them in boiling water for 10 minutes or until softened. Drain well; dry with paper towels before using.

1. Preheat oven to 350°F. Insert sharp thin knife (utility knife) from each end of roast through center of large muscle and twist to form a tube the length of roast. Push prunes into tube.

2. Place roast on rack in roasting pan. Roast 45 to 50 minutes or until temperature of pork reaches 145°F on instant-read thermometer.

3. Heat preserves in small saucepan until slightly melted; stir in mustard and pepper. Brush half of preserves mixture over pork. Roast 15 to 20 minutes or until temperature reaches 155°F, brushing remaining preserves mixture over pork after 10 minutes. Let stand 10 to 15 minutes before slicing.   *Makes 6 to 8 servings*

Saucy Mario Sandwiches

 1 pound ground beef
 2 cups PREGO® Traditional Italian Sauce, any variety
 ¼ cup grated Parmesan cheese
 6 PEPPERIDGE FARM® Classic Hamburger Buns, split

1. Cook the beef in a 10-inch skillet over medium-high heat until the beef is well browned, stirring frequently to separate meat. Pour off any fat.

2. Stir the sauce and cheese into the skillet. Cook until the mixture is hot and bubbling.

3. Divide the beef mixture among the buns.   *Makes 6 servings*

Prep Time: 5 minutes • **Cook Time:** 15 minutes

Grilled Garlic-Pepper Shrimp

⅓ **cup olive oil**
2 **tablespoons lemon juice**
1 **teaspoon garlic-pepper blend**
20 **jumbo raw shrimp, peeled and deveined**
Lemon wedges (optional)

1. Combine oil, lemon juice and garlic-pepper in large resealable food storage bag; add shrimp. Marinate in refrigerator 20 to 30 minutes, turning bag once.

2. Meanwhile, spray grid with nonstick cooking spray. Prepare grill for direct cooking.

3. Thread 5 shrimp onto each of 4 skewers;* discard marinade. Grill over medium heat 6 minutes or until pink and opaque. Serve with lemon wedges, if desired.   *Makes 4 servings*

*If using wooden skewers, soak in water at least 20 minutes before using to prevent scorching.

Roasted Almond Tilapia

2 **tilapia or Boston scrod fillets (6 ounces each)**
¼ **teaspoon salt**
1 **tablespoon prepared mustard**
¼ **cup whole wheat bread crumbs**
2 **tablespoons chopped almonds**
Paprika (optional)
Lemon wedges (optional)

1. Preheat oven to 450°F. Place fish on small baking sheet; season with salt. Spread mustard over fish. Combine bread crumbs and almonds in small bowl; sprinkle over fish. Press crumbs lightly to adhere. Sprinkle with paprika, if desired.

2. Bake 8 to 10 minutes or until fish is opaque in center and begins to flake when tested with fork. Serve with lemon wedges, if desired.
                                        Makes 2 servings

113

Spinach and Mushroom Frittata

Vegetable cooking spray
10 eggs
1 can (10¾ ounces) CAMPBELL'S® Condensed Cream of Mushroom Soup (Regular or 98% Fat Free)
1 package (10 ounces) frozen chopped spinach, thawed and well drained
1½ cups shredded Swiss cheese or Jarlsberg cheese (about 6 ounces)
½ teaspoon ground black pepper

1. Heat the oven to 375°F. Spray a 2-quart shallow baking dish with the cooking spray.

2. Beat the eggs in a large bowl with a fork or whisk. Stir in the soup. Stir in the spinach, **1 cup** of the cheese and black pepper. Pour the egg mixture into the baking dish.

3. Bake for 35 minutes or until the eggs are set. Sprinkle with the remaining cheese. *Makes 8 servings*

Kitchen Tip: You can prepare the frittata as directed above, then cover and refrigerate for up to 24 hours. Before serving, remove the frittata from the refrigerator and let stand for about 30 minutes. Heat the oven to 350°F. Bake for 20 minutes or until hot.

Prep Time: 10 minutes • **Bake Time:** 35 minutes

Sweet 'n' Spicy Chicken

1 bottle (8 ounces) WISH-BONE® Russian Dressing
1 envelope LIPTON® RECIPE SECRETS® Onion Soup Mix
1 jar (12 ounces) apricot preserves
1 (2½- to 3-pound) chicken, cut into serving pieces

1. Preheat oven to 425°F. In small bowl, combine Wish-Bone Russian Dressing, soup mix and preserves.

2. In 13×9-inch baking dish, arrange chicken; pour dressing mixture over chicken. Bake uncovered, basting occasionally, 40 minutes or until chicken is thoroughly cooked. Serve, if desired, with hot cooked rice. *Makes 6 servings*

Grilled Reuben Burger

1½ **pounds ground beef**
½ **cup shredded Swiss cheese (about 2 ounces)**
½ **cup water**
1 **envelope LIPTON® RECIPE SECRETS® Onion Soup Mix***
1 **tablespoon crisp-cooked crumbled bacon or bacon bits**
½ **teaspoon caraway seeds (optional)**

*Also terrific with LIPTON® RECIPE SECRETS® Onion Mushroom Soup Mix.

1. In large bowl, combine all ingredients; shape into 6 patties.

2. Grill or broil until done. Top, if desired, with heated sauerkraut and additional bacon. *Makes 6 servings*

Orange-Glazed Game Hens

4 **TYSON® Cornish Game Hens, thawed**
1 **teaspoon salt**
¼ **teaspoon black pepper**
½ **cup frozen orange juice concentrate, thawed**
¼ **cup ketchup**
¼ **cup honey**

1. Preheat oven to 375°F. Wash hands. Rinse hens with cold water and pat dry with paper towels. Sprinkle hens with salt and pepper; place in oiled roasting pan. Wash hands.

2. Roast hens 30 minutes. Combine orange juice concentrate, ketchup and honey. Baste hens with glaze. Roast, basting every 10 minutes, 40 minutes longer or until internal juices of chicken run clear. (Or insert instant-read meat thermometer into thickest part of chicken. Temperature should read 180°F.) Let stand 10 minutes before serving. Refrigerate leftovers immediately.

Makes 8 servings

Serving Suggestion: Serve with buttered potatoes and asparagus.

Prep Time: 10 minutes • **Cook Time:** 70 minutes

Grilled Reuben Burger

Olive Lover's Pasta

1 jar (1 pound 10 ounces) RAGÚ® ROBUSTO!® Pasta Sauce
1 package (12 ounces) tri-color pasta twists, cooked and drained
1 cup sliced assorted pitted olives
2 tablespoons grated Parmesan cheese

1. In 2-quart saucepan, heat Pasta Sauce over medium-low heat.

2. To serve, toss hot pasta with Pasta Sauce and olives, then sprinkle with cheese. *Makes 6 servings*

Prep Time: 20 minutes • **Cook Time:** 5 minutes

Stovetop Tuna Casserole

1 package (12 ounces) deluxe macaroni and cheese dinner with shell pasta
2 cups frozen peas
1 tablespoon butter
½ teaspoon hot pepper sauce
1 can (6 ounces) chunk white tuna

1. Remove cheese sauce pouch from macaroni and cheese; set aside. Bring 6 cups cold water to a boil in large saucepan. Stir in pasta. Cook 6 to 8 minutes or until pasta is tender.

2. Meanwhile, bring 4 cups cold water to a boil in medium saucepan. Stir in peas. Cook 3 to 5 minutes or until tender.

3. Drain pasta and return to saucepan. Stir in reserved cheese sauce, butter and hot pepper sauce until well blended. Drain tuna and flake with fork. Stir into pasta. Drain peas and stir into pasta. *Makes 4 servings*

Variation: Preheat oven to 350°F. Spray 8-inch baking dish with nonstick cooking spray. Spread tuna casserole mixture in prepared baking dish; sprinkle with 1½ cups crushed potato chips or buttery round crackers. Bake 12 to 15 minutes or until topping is lightly browned.

On the Side

Chive & Onion Mashed Potatoes

2 pounds potatoes, peeled, quartered (about 6 cups)
½ cup milk
1 tub (8 ounces) PHILADELPHIA® Chive & Onion Cream Cheese Spread
¼ cup KRAFT® Ranch Dressing

BRING potatoes and enough water to cover in 3-quart saucepan. Bring to a boil.

REDUCE heat to medium; cook 20 to 25 minutes or until tender. Drain.

MASH potatoes, gradually stirring in milk, cream cheese spread and dressing until light and fluffy. Serve immediately.

Makes 10 servings (½ cup each)

Make Ahead: Mix ingredients as directed; spoon into 1½-quart casserole dish. Cover. Refrigerate several hours or overnight. When ready to serve, bake, uncovered, at 350°F 1 hour or until heated through.

Substitute: Substitute KRAFT® Three Cheese Ranch Dressing for Ranch Dressing.

Prep Time: 10 minutes • **Cook Time:** 25 minutes

Prosciutto Provolone Rolls

1 loaf (1 pound) frozen bread dough, thawed
¼ cup garlic and herb spreadable cheese
6 thin slices prosciutto (about 1 (3-ounce) package)
6 slices provolone cheese

1. Spray 12 standard (2½-inch) muffin cups with nonstick cooking spray. Roll out dough on lightly floured surface into 12×10-inch rectangle.

2. Spread garlic and herb cheese evenly over dough. Arrange prosciutto slices over herb cheese; top with provolone slices. Starting with long side, roll.up dough jelly-roll style; pinch seam to seal.

3. Cut crosswise into 1-inch slices; arrange slices, cut side down, in prepared muffin cups. Cover and let rise in warm, draft-free place 30 to 40 minutes or until nearly doubled in bulk. Preheat oven to 350°F.

4. Bake rolls about 18 minutes or until golden brown. Loosen edges of rolls with knife; remove from pan to wire rack. Serve warm.

Makes 12 rolls

Salsa-Buttered Corn on the Cob

6 ears fresh corn, shucked
4 tablespoons butter, softened
¼ cup ORTEGA® Salsa
2 tablespoons ORTEGA® Taco Seasoning Mix, or to taste

Bring large pot of water to a boil. Add corn; cook 5 to 10 minutes.

Combine butter and salsa in small bowl; mix well. Place seasoning mix in another small bowl. Spread salsa butter onto cooked corn and sprinkle on seasoning mix, to taste. *Makes 6 servings*

Tip: For a different side dish, cut the corn off the cob and heat in a skillet with the salsa butter and taco seasoning mix.

Prep Time: 5 minutes • **Start to Finish Time:** 20 minutes

Asparagus Bundles with Prosciutto & Goat Cheese

REYNOLDS WRAP® Heavy Duty Aluminum Foil
1 pound fresh asparagus, trimmed
2 thin slices prosciutto, cut into 1-inch-wide strips
1 tablespoon olive oil
¼ teaspoon salt
⅛ teaspoon freshly ground black pepper
2 tablespoons chopped roasted red peppers
¼ cup crumbled goat or feta cheese

Preheat oven to 450°F. Line a 15×10×1-inch baking pan with Reynolds Wrap Heavy Duty Aluminum Foil.

Wrap bundles of 3 or 4 asparagus spears around the middle with a strip of prosciutto. Place bundles in a single layer in foil-lined pan. Drizzle olive oil over asparagus bundles. Sprinkle with salt and pepper. Top with roasted red peppers.

Bake 6 to 8 minutes or until asparagus is crisp-tender. Sprinkle with cheese.

Continue baking 5 minutes longer or until cheese is softened and heated through. *Makes 6 servings*

Prep Time: 8 minutes • **Cook Time:** 11 minutes

Cranberry Crunch Gelatin

2 cups boiling water
2 packages (4-serving size each) cherry-flavored gelatin
1 can (16 ounces) whole berry cranberry sauce
1½ cups mini marshmallows
1 cup coarsely chopped walnuts

1. Stir boiling water into gelatin in large bowl; stir 2 minutes or until completely dissolved. Chill about 2 hours or until slightly set.

2. Fold cranberry sauce, marshmallows and walnuts into gelatin mixture. Pour into 6-cup gelatin mold. Cover and refrigerate at least 4 hours or until set. Remove from mold. *Makes 8 servings*

Polenta au Gratin

1 cup PACE® Picante Sauce
1 package (18 ounces) prepared polenta, cut into ½-inch slices
4 green onions, minced (about ½ cup)
1½ cups shredded Mexican cheese blend (about 6 ounces)

1. Heat the oven to 350°F. Spread ½ **cup** picante sauce on the bottom of a 2-quart shallow baking dish. Layer the polenta slices, overlapping slightly, in the baking dish. Top with the green onions, remaining picante sauce and cheese.

2. Bake for 25 minutes or until the polenta is golden brown and the cheese is melted. Let stand for 5 minutes.   *Makes 6 servings*

Prep Time: 10 minutes • **Bake Time:** 25 minutes •
Stand Time: 5 minutes

Kale with Caramelized Garlic

1½ pounds fresh kale, tough stems removed and discarded, leaves thinly sliced (16 cups)
2 cups water
1 tablespoon olive oil
8 cloves garlic, thinly sliced
1 teaspoon red wine vinegar
¼ teaspoon salt
⅛ to ¼ teaspoon red pepper flakes

1. Place kale and water in large saucepan; bring to a boil over medium-high heat. Cover and cook 6 to 8 minutes or until kale is tender but still bright green. Drain in colander.

2. Meanwhile, heat oil in large nonstick skillet over medium heat. Add garlic; cook and stir about 4 minutes or until garlic is golden brown, being careful not to allow garlic to burn. Add kale, vinegar, salt and red pepper flakes; mix well.

Makes 4 to 6 servings

Broccoli Italian Style

1¼ **pounds fresh broccoli**
2 **tablespoons lemon juice**
1 **tablespoon extra virgin olive oil**
1 **clove garlic, minced**
1 **teaspoon chopped fresh parsley**
   Dash black pepper

1. Trim broccoli, discarding tough stems. Cut broccoli into florets with 2-inch stems. Cut remaining broccoli stems into ½-inch slices.

2. Bring 1 quart water to a boil in large saucepan over medium-high heat. Add broccoli; return to a boil. Cook, uncovered, 3 to 5 minutes or until broccoli is fork-tender. Drain and transfer to serving dish.

3. Combine lemon juice, oil, garlic, parsley and pepper in small bowl. Pour over broccoli; toss to coat. Let stand, covered, 1 to 2 hours before serving to allow flavors to blend.

Makes 4 servings

Mediterranean Couscous Salad

2 **cups water**
½ **teaspoon salt**
1 **package (10 ounces) couscous**
¼ **cup WISH-BONE® Robusto Italian Dressing**
1 **jar (4 ounces) chopped pimentos, drained**
1 **cup firmly packed shredded baby spinach leaves**

Bring water and salt to a boil in 2-quart saucepan over high heat. Remove from heat and stir in couscous. Let stand, covered, 5 minutes.

Fluff couscous with fork. Stir in remaining ingredients.

Makes 10 servings

Prep Time: 10 minutes • **Cook Time:** 5 minutes

Pizza Biscuits

2½ **cups baking mix**
1 **cup CABOT® Sour Cream**
4 **ounces CABOT® Sharp Cheddar, grated (1 cup)**
½ **cup chopped cooked ham**

1. Preheat oven to 400°F.

2. In mixing bowl, combine baking mix, sour cream, cheese and ham; stir together to form soft dough.

3. Turn dough out onto lightly floured work surface and pat into ¾-inch-thick layer. Cut out biscuits with cutter. Place on baking sheet.

4. Bake for 12 to 15 minutes or until golden brown; serve hot.

Makes about 12 biscuits

Garlic Fries

1 **envelope LIPTON® RECIPE SECRETS® Savory Herb with Garlic Soup Mix***
1 **cup plain dry bread crumbs**
2 **pounds large red or all-purpose potatoes, cut lengthwise into wedges**
⅓ **cup I CAN'T BELIEVE IT'S NOT BUTTER!® Spread, melted**

*Also terrific with LIPTON® RECIPE SECRETS® Onion Soup Mix.

1. Preheat oven to 400°F. In large bowl, blend soup mix with bread crumbs. Dip potatoes in I Can't Believe It's Not Butter!® Spread, then soup mixture, until evenly coated.

2. In 15½×10½×1-inch jelly-roll pan sprayed with nonstick cooking spray, arrange potatoes in single layer.

3. Bake uncovered 40 minutes or until potatoes are tender and golden brown.

Makes 4 servings

Honey-Lemon Green and Yellow Beans

1 pound green beans
1 pound yellow wax beans
2 tablespoons butter
2 tablespoons honey
1 tablespoon grated lemon peel
1 teaspoon salt
½ teaspoon black pepper

1. Bring 2½ quarts salted water to a boil in large saucepan. Add beans; boil 2 minutes. Remove immediately to bowl of ice water. Drain and pat dry.*

2. Melt butter in large nonstick skillet over medium-high heat. Add beans; cook and stir 2 minutes or until heated through. Add honey; cook 1 minute. Remove from heat; stir in lemon peel, salt and pepper. Serve immediately. *Makes 8 servings*

This can be done several hours ahead. Cover and refrigerate beans until ready to use.

Crispy Skillet Potatoes

2 tablespoons olive oil
4 small red potatoes, cut into thin wedges
½ cup chopped onion
2 tablespoons lemon pepper
½ teaspoon salt
2 tablespoons chopped fresh parsley

1. Heat oil in large skillet over medium heat. Add potatoes, onion, lemon pepper and salt; stir to combine.

2. Cover and cook 25 to 30 minutes or until potatoes are tender and browned, turning occasionally. Sprinkle with parsley.
Makes 4 servings

Smokin' Chipotle Coleslaw

1 bag (16 ounces) coleslaw mix
1 packet (1.25 ounces) ORTEGA® Chipotle Seasoning Mix
1 cup mayonnaise
½ cup ORTEGA® Salsa, any variety
Salt, to taste

Toss coleslaw mix and seasoning mix in large bowl. Fold in mayonnaise and salsa until well combined. Season with salt, if desired.   *Makes 6 servings*

Tip: For an even crunchier salad, try adding sliced radishes to the slaw. Or serve on beef, chicken or turkey tacos for added zest.

Prep Time: 5 minutes • **Start to Finish Time:** 5 minutes

◎◎◎

Double Onion Crunchy Rings

2 cups *French's*® French Fried Onions
¼ cup plus 2 tablespoons all-purpose flour, divided
2 cups medium onions, cut into ½-inch rings
2 egg whites, beaten

1. Heat oven to 400°F. Place French Fried Onions and 2 tablespoons flour in plastic bag. Lightly crush with hands or with rolling pin. Place remaining ¼ cup flour in separate plastic bag. Toss onion rings in ¼ cup flour; shake off excess.

2. Dip floured onion rings into beaten egg whites. Coat with crushed onions, pressing firmly to adhere.

3. Place rings on lightly greased baking rack set over rimmed baking sheet. Bake 10 minutes or until onions are tender.
Makes about 2½ dozen pieces

Prep Time: 15 minutes • **Cook Time:** 10 minutes

Thyme-Scented Roasted Sweet Potatoes and Onions

**2 large sweet potatoes (about 1¼ pounds), unpeeled and
    scrubbed**
1 medium sweet or yellow onion, cut into chunks
2 tablespoons canola oil
1 teaspoon dried thyme
½ teaspoon salt
½ teaspoon smoked paprika
⅛ teaspoon ground red pepper (optional)

1. Preheat oven to 425°F. Spray 15×10-inch jelly-roll pan with
nonstick cooking spray.

2. Cut sweet potatoes into 1-inch chunks; place in large bowl.
Add onion, oil, thyme, salt, paprika and red pepper, if desired;
toss to coat. Spread vegetables in single layer on prepared pan.

3. Bake 20 to 25 minutes or until very tender, stirring after
10 minutes. Let stand 5 minutes before serving.

Makes 6 to 8 servings

Fiery Creamed Spinach

1 tablespoon olive oil
1 onion, sliced
1 bag (12 ounces) spinach, washed and chopped
¾ cup milk
**1 packet (1.25 ounces) ORTEGA® Hot and Spicy Taco
    Seasoning Mix**

Heat oil in large skillet over medium heat. Add onion. Cook and
stir 4 minutes or until translucent.

Add spinach. Cook and stir until spinach begins to wilt. Stir in milk
and seasoning mix. Cook and stir 4 minutes or until sauce thickens.
Serve warm. *Makes 4 servings*

Tip: For a quick and healthy snack, serve Fiery Creamed Spinach
wrapped in a soft flour tortilla.

Prep Time: 5 minutes • **Start to Finish Time:** 15 minutes

Chutney Glazed Carrots

2 cups cut peeled carrots (1½-inch pieces)
3 tablespoons cranberry or mango chutney
1 tablespoon Dijon mustard
2 teaspoons butter
2 tablespoons chopped pecans, toasted*

*Toast pecans in a dry skillet over medium heat for 3 to 5 minutes or until fragrant, stirring occasionally.

1. Place carrots in medium saucepan; cover with water. Bring to a boil over high heat. Reduce heat; simmer 6 to 8 minutes or until carrots are tender.

2. Drain carrots; return to pan. Add chutney, mustard and butter; cook and stir over medium heat about 2 minutes or until carrots are glazed. Top with pecans. *Makes 4 servings*

Mexican Corn Casserole

Vegetable cooking spray
1 can (10¾ ounces) CAMPBELL'S® Condensed Cheddar Cheese Soup
1 cup PACE® Chunky Salsa
1 bag (16 ounces) frozen whole kernel corn, thawed (about 4 cups)
1 cup coarsely crushed tortilla chips

1. Spray a 2-quart casserole with the cooking spray. Stir the soup, salsa and corn into the prepared dish. Sprinkle the tortilla chips over the corn mixture.

2. Bake at 350°F for 30 minutes or until hot and bubbly. Serve immediately. *Makes 6 servings*

Prep Time: 5 minutes • **Bake Time:** 30 minutes

No-Fuss Finales

Toffee Chocolate Crispies

1 cup slivered almonds
1 cup crisp rice cereal
½ cup milk chocolate toffee bits
1 cup milk or semisweet chocolate chips
1 teaspoon shortening

1. Line baking sheet or large tray with foil. Place almonds in medium nonstick skillet; toast over medium heat, stirring frequently, 7 to 8 minutes or until lightly browned. Pour almonds into large bowl; stir in cereal and toffee bits.

2. Place chocolate chips and shortening in medium microwavable bowl. Microwave on HIGH 30 seconds; stir to blend. Microwave 20 seconds more; stir until smooth. Pour chocolate mixture over almond mixture; stir until evenly coated.

3. Drop mixture by rounded tablespoonfuls onto prepared baking sheet. Refrigerate 30 minutes or until cool and solid. Serve immediately or store between layers of waxed paper in airtight container in refrigerator up to 1 week.

Makes about 27 candies

◎◎◎

For an even more intensely chocolate
treat, use chocolate-flavored crisp
rice cereal instead of plain.

Lemony Blueberry Cheese Tart

1 (9-inch) frozen pie crust, thawed
1 (8-ounce) container mascarpone cheese or 1 (8-ounce)
    package cream cheese, softened
5 tablespoons lemon curd,* divided
2 cups fresh blueberries

*Lemon curd can be found in the jam and jelly section of the
supermarket.*

Preheat oven to 375°F. Press the pie crust into a 9-inch tart
pan with removable bottom, or leave in the aluminum pie
tin. With the tines of a fork, pierce the bottom and side. Bake
until lightly browned, about 10 minutes; refrigerate until cool,
about 10 minutes. In a small bowl, stir together cheese and
3 tablespoons of the lemon curd until smooth. (If mixture is too
thick to spread, stir in a small amount of milk.) Spread mixture in
the bottom of the cooled tart shell. In a medium bowl, gently
stir the blueberries and the remaining 2 tablespoons lemon curd
until thoroughly combined. Spoon the blueberries evenly over the
cheese layer. Cover and chill 2 hours. To serve, remove the side of
the tart pan if used; cut into wedges.   *Makes 8 servings*

*Favorite recipe from **U.S. Highbush Blueberry Council***

Chocolate Satin Pie

1 can (12 fluid ounces) NESTLÉ® CARNATION® Evaporated Milk
2 large egg yolks
2 cups (12-ounce package) NESTLÉ® TOLL HOUSE® Semi-Sweet
    Chocolate Morsels
1 *prepared* 9-inch (6 ounces) graham cracker crumb crust
    Whipped cream (optional)
¼ cup chopped nuts (optional)

WHISK together evaporated milk and egg yolks in medium
saucepan. Heat over medium-low heat, stirring constantly, until
mixture is very hot and thickens slightly; do not boil. Remove from
heat; stir in morsels until completely melted and mixture is smooth.

POUR into crust; refrigerate for 3 hours or until firm. Top with
whipped cream before serving; sprinkle with nuts.

Makes 10 servings

Cinnamon-Sugar Knots

¼ cup sugar
¾ teaspoon ground cinnamon
1 package (about 18 ounces) spice cake mix
1 package (8 ounces) cream cheese, softened

1. Preheat oven to 350°F. Combine sugar and cinnamon in small bowl.

2. Beat cake mix and cream cheese in large bowl with electric mixer at medium speed until well blended. Shape dough into 1-inch balls; roll each ball into log about 4 inches long. Gently coil dough and pull up ends to form knot. Place about 1½ inches apart on ungreased cookie sheets. Sprinkle with cinnamon-sugar.

3. Bake 10 to 12 minutes or until edges are lightly browned. Cool on cookie sheets 2 minutes. Remove to wire rack. Serve warm or cool completely. *Makes about 4 dozen cookies*

Pomegranate Peach-Sicles

1 jar (24.5 ounces) DOLE® Sliced Peaches
2 cups vanilla low-fat yogurt
¼ cup sugar
12 (5-ounce) paper cups
12 wooden ice cream sticks
2 cups pomegranate juice, chilled

• Drain peach slices, reserving ½ cup syrup.

• Combine peaches, yogurt and sugar in blender or food processor container. Cover; blend until smooth. Pour mixture evenly into 12 paper cups. Place on tray and freeze about 1 hour or until partially set.

• Insert one wooden stick into center of each cup; freeze 1 hour longer or until almost solid.

• Pour pomegranate juice evenly into each cup over yogurt mixture. Freeze until firm, 2 hours or overnight. Remove paper cups to serve. *Makes 12 servings*

Individual Chocolate Soufflés

2 tablespoons plus 1 teaspoon butter, divided
2 tablespoons plus ½ teaspoon sugar, divided
4 ounces bittersweet chocolate, broken into pieces
2 eggs, separated, at room temperature
Powdered sugar (optional)

1. Preheat oven to 375°F. Use 1 teaspoon cold butter to coat 2 (¾-cup) ramekins or soufflé dishes. Add ½ teaspoon sugar to ramekins; shake to coat bottoms and sides.

2. Combine chocolate and remaining 2 tablespoons butter in top of double boiler. Heat over simmering water until chocolate is melted and smooth, stirring occasionally. Remove from heat; stir in egg yolks, 1 at a time. (Mixture may become grainy but will smooth out with addition of egg whites.)

3. Beat egg whites in medium bowl with electric mixer at high speed until soft peaks form. Gradually add remaining 2 tablespoons sugar; continue beating until stiff peaks form and mixture is glossy.

4. Gently fold egg whites into chocolate mixture. Do not overmix; allow some white streaks to remain. Divide batter evenly between prepared ramekins.

5. Bake 15 minutes or until soufflés rise but remain moist in centers. Sprinkle with powdered sugar, if desired. Serve immediately.

Makes 2 soufflés

◎◎◎

Add a pinch of cream of tartar to the
egg whites before beating to make
a stronger egg white foam.

Quick Pumpkin Gingerbread

1 package (14½ ounces) gingerbread mix
½ (15-ounce) can solid-pack pumpkin
½ cup orange juice
1 egg
Cream cheese (optional)

1. Preheat oven to 350°F. Spray 9×5-inch loaf pan with nonstick cooking spray.

2. Beat gingerbread mix, pumpkin, orange juice and egg in medium bowl with electric mixer at medium speed until blended. Pour into prepared pan.

3. Bake 35 to 37 minutes or until toothpick inserted into center comes out clean. Cool in pan on wire rack 10 minutes. Remove from pan; cool completely on wire rack. Serve with cream cheese, if desired.   *Makes about 8 servings*

Peanut Butter & Jelly Ice Cream Sandwiches

8 slices (½-inch-thick) store-bought pound cake, toasted
¼ cup SKIPPY® Creamy Peanut Butter
¼ cup raspberry jam
1 cup BREYERS® All Natural Vanilla or French Vanilla Ice Cream, slightly softened

On cookie sheet, arrange cake slices. Evenly spread Peanut Butter on 4 slices, then spread jam on remaining slices. Freeze 10 minutes or until firm.

On Peanut Butter-covered slices, evenly spread BREYERS® All Natural Vanilla Ice Cream, then top with remaining slices, jam-side-down, pressing slightly. Freeze 10 minutes or until ready to serve. To serve, diagonally cut each "sandwich" in half.   *Makes 4 servings*

Prep Time: 10 minutes • **Freeze Time:** 20 minutes

Mini Chocolate Pies

1 package (4-serving size) vanilla cook & serve pudding and pie filling mix*

1 cup HERSHEY'S Mini Chips Semi-Sweet Chocolate

1 package (4 ounces) single-serve graham cracker crusts (6 crusts)

Whipped topping (optional)

Additional HERSHEY'S Mini Chips Semi-Sweet Chocolate, HERSHEY'S SPECIAL DARK® Chocolate Chips or HERSHEY'S Semi-Sweet Chocolate Chips (optional)

*Do not use instant pudding mix.

1. Prepare pudding and pie filling mix as directed on package; remove from heat. Immediately add 1 cup small chocolate chips; stir until melted. Cool 5 minutes, stirring occasionally.

2. Pour filling into crusts; press plastic wrap directly onto surface. Refrigerate several hours or until firm. Garnish with whipped topping and small chocolate chips.   *Makes 6 servings*

Whole Grain Rice Pudding

1 cup MINUTE® Brown Rice, uncooked

1½ cups milk

⅓ cup maple syrup or honey

1 tablespoon butter

½ teaspoon ground cinnamon, nutmeg or allspice

Fresh mint leaves (optional)

Prepare rice according to package directions.

Combine rice, milk and maple syrup in medium saucepan. Bring to a boil; reduce heat and simmer 20 minutes, stirring frequently.

Remove from heat and stir in butter and cinnamon. Garnish with additional cinnamon and mint leaves, if desired.

Makes 4 servings

Watermelon Granita

5 cups cubed seeded watermelon
½ cup sugar
1 envelope (¼ ounce) unflavored gelatin
½ cup cranberry juice cocktail

1. Process watermelon in food processor until nearly smooth. (You should have about 3⅓ cups.)

2. Combine sugar and gelatin in small saucepan. Gradually stir in juice. Cook and stir over low heat until gelatin dissolves. Add to watermelon purée in food processor; process until combined. Pour into 8-inch square baking dish. Cover and freeze about 5 hours or until firm.

3. Break watermelon mixture into chunks. Return to baking dish. Freeze about 3 hours or until firm. To serve, stir and scrape granita with fork to create icy texture. Spoon into dessert dishes.

Makes 6 to 8 servings

Triple-Layer Lemon Pie

2 cups cold milk
2 packages (4-serving size each) JELL-O® Lemon Flavor Instant Pudding & Pie Filling
1 HONEY MAID® Graham Pie Crust (6 ounces)
1 tub (8 ounces) COOL WHIP® Whipped Topping, thawed, divided
Lemon peel, optional

POUR milk into large bowl. Add dry pudding mixes. Beat with wire whisk 2 minutes or until well blended. (Mixture will be thick.)

SPREAD 1½ cups of the pudding onto bottom of crust; set aside. Add half of the whipped topping to remaining pudding; stir gently until well blended. Spread over pudding layer in crust; top with the remaining whipped topping.

REFRIGERATE 3 hours or until set. Garnish with lemon peel, if desired. Store leftover pie in refrigerator. *Makes 8 servings*

Jazz It Up: Garnish with ½ cup fresh raspberries or sliced strawberries just before serving.

White Chocolate Lace Cups

2 squares BAKER'S® Premium White Baking Chocolate
2 teaspoons grated orange peel
¼ cup thawed COOL WHIP® Whipped Topping
¼ cup raspberries

LINE each of 2 medium muffin cups with a piece of foil. Place in freezer 5 minutes. Meanwhile, microwave chocolate in small microwavable bowl on medium (50%) 1½ minutes; stir until chocolate is completely melted.

DRIZZLE chocolate with a spoon onto bottoms and up sides of prepared muffin cups. Freeze 5 minutes. Carefully remove foil cups from pan; gently peel off and discard foil.

STIR orange peel into whipped topping; spoon evenly into chocolate cups. Top with raspberries.

Makes 2 servings (1 filled chocolate cup each)

Make Ahead: Unfilled chocolate cups can be stored in the freezer for up to 3 months. Remove from the freezer and fill as directed just before serving.

Prep Time: 15 minutes • **Total time:** 15 minutes

Coconut Custard

4 cups coconut milk
⅔ cup ARGO® Corn Starch
2 cups KARO® Light Corn Syrup
¼ teaspoon salt
Ground cinnamon

1. In medium saucepan, stir 1 cup coconut milk into corn starch until dissolved.

2. Add remaining coconut milk, corn syrup and salt. Cook over medium-high heat until boiling, stirring constantly until mixture thickens.

3. Pour into individual serving dishes. Sprinkle with cinnamon and refrigerate to chill.

Makes 10 servings

Pumpkin Custard

2 cups milk
⅓ cup CREAM OF WHEAT® Cinnamon Swirl Instant Hot Cereal,
      uncooked
½ cup canned pumpkin pie mix
1 teaspoon ground cinnamon
   Whipped cream (optional)
   Toasted pecans (optional)

1. Bring milk to a boil in saucepan over medium-high heat. Turn down heat; stir in Cream of Wheat. Cook and stir until thickened, about 5 minutes.

2. Add pumpkin pie mix and stir until well combined. Let stand 10 minutes. Spoon into 4 small ramekins. Refrigerate at least 1 hour. Sprinkle with cinnamon and serve with whipped cream and toasted pecans, if desired.   *Makes 4 servings*

Tip: To toast pecans, spread in single layer in heavy-bottomed skillet. Cook over medium heat 1 to 2 minutes, stirring frequently, until nuts are lightly browned. Remove from skillet immediately. Cool before using.

Tip: This dessert is also delicious served warm, right after you make it. You can prepare it in the time it takes to make coffee.

◎◎◎
In addition to creating delicious desserts,
Cream of Wheat is also a good source
of calcium and iron.

5 Ingredient
cookbook

Contents

Chorizo & Caramelized
Onion Tortilla

¼ **cup olive oil**
3 **medium yellow onions, quartered and sliced**
½ **pound Spanish-style fully cooked chorizo (about 2 links)**
    or andouille sausage, diced
6 **eggs**
    Salt and black pepper
½ **cup chopped fresh parsley**

1. Heat oil in medium skillet over medium heat. Add onions; cook, covered, 10 minutes or until onions are translucent. Reduce heat to low; cook, uncovered, 40 minutes or until golden and very tender. Remove onions from skillet and set aside to cool.

2. Add chorizo to same skillet. Cook over medium heat, stirring occasionally, 5 minutes or just until chorizo begins to brown. Remove chorizo from skillet; set aside to cool.

3. Preheat oven to 350°F. Spray 9-inch square baking pan with olive oil cooking spray.

4. Whisk eggs in medium bowl; season with salt and pepper. Add onions, chorizo and parsley; stir gently until well blended. Pour egg mixture into prepared pan.

5. Bake 12 to 15 minutes or until center is almost set. *Turn oven to broil.* Broil 1 to 2 minutes or just until top starts to brown. Transfer pan to wire rack; cool completely. Cut into triangles; serve at room temperature or chilled. *Makes 32 triangles*

Tip: The tortilla can be made up to 1 day ahead and refrigerated until serving. To serve at room temperature, remove from refrigerator 30 minutes before serving.

Mexican Drumsticks with Ranchero Dipping Sauce

12 chicken drumsticks (about 3 pounds)
1 packet (1.25 ounces) ORTEGA® Taco Seasoning Mix
1 bottle (8 ounces) ORTEGA® Taco Sauce
1 bottle (8 ounces) ranch dressing
1 cup ORTEGA® Original Salsa

Preheat oven to 350°F. Arrange drumsticks on baking pan. Sprinkle seasoning mix over drumsticks, turning to coat both sides.

Bake 45 minutes; turn drumsticks over halfway through to bake evenly. Remove from oven.

Place taco sauce in large mixing bowl. Add drumsticks and toss to coat evenly. Replace on baking sheet; broil 4 minutes on each side or until crisp.

Combine ranch dressing and salsa to make dipping sauce. Serve with warm drumsticks. *Makes 12 appetizers*

Tip: Experiment with different flavors of ORTEGA® taco sauce for a spicier taste. Or try this recipe with chicken wings for a great alternative to traditional hot wings.

Margherita Panini Bites

1 loaf (16 ounces) ciabatta or crusty Italian bread, cut into 16 (½-inch) slices
8 teaspoons pesto
16 fresh basil leaves
8 slices mozzarella cheese
24 thin slices plum tomato (about 3 tomatoes)
1 tablespoon olive oil

1. Preheat grill or broiler. Spread one side of 8 bread slices with 1 teaspoon pesto. Top each with 2 basil leaves, 1 mozzarella slice and 3 tomato slices. Top with remaining bread slices.

2. Brush both sides of sandwiches lightly with oil. Grill sandwiches 5 minutes or until lightly browned and cheese is melted. Cut each sandwich into 4 pieces. Serve warm. *Makes 32 panini bites*

Chipotle Chicken Quesadillas

1 package (8 ounces) cream cheese, softened
1 cup (4 ounces) shredded Mexican cheese blend
1 tablespoon minced chipotle pepper in adobo sauce
5 (10-inch) flour tortillas
5 cups shredded cooked chicken (about 1¼ pounds)

1. Combine cheeses and pepper in large bowl.

2. Spread ⅓ cup cheese mixture over half of one tortilla. Top with about 1 cup chicken. Fold over tortilla. Repeat with remaining cheese mixture, tortillas and chicken.

3. Heat large nonstick skillet over medium-high heat. Spray outside surface of tortillas with nonstick cooking spray. Cook quesadillas 4 to 6 minutes or until lightly browned, turning once during cooking.

4. Cut each quesadilla into 4 wedges.   *Makes 5 servings*

Serving Suggestion: Serve with guacamole, sour cream, salsa and chopped fresh cilantro.

Mini Chickpea Cakes

1 can (about 15 ounces) chickpeas, rinsed and drained
1 cup shredded carrots
⅓ cup seasoned dry bread crumbs
¼ cup creamy Italian salad dressing, plus additional for serving
1 egg

1. Preheat oven to 375°F. Spray baking sheets with nonstick cooking spray.

2. Coarsely mash chickpeas in medium bowl with potato masher. Stir in carrots, bread crumbs, ¼ cup salad dressing and egg; mix well.

3. Shape chickpea mixture into 24 patties, using about 1 tablespoon mixture for each. Place on prepared baking sheets.

4. Bake 15 to 18 minutes or until chickpea cakes are lightly browned on both sides, turning halfway through baking time. Serve warm with additional salad dressing for dipping.   *Makes 24 cakes*

Pineapple-Scallop Bites

½ cup *French's*® Honey Dijon Mustard
¼ cup orange marmalade
1 cup canned pineapple cubes (24 pieces)
12 sea scallops (8 ounces), cut in half crosswise
12 strips (6 ounces) uncooked turkey bacon,* cut in half
    crosswise

Or substitute thinly-sliced regular bacon for turkey bacon.

1. Soak 12 (6-inch) bamboo skewers in hot water 20 minutes.
Combine mustard and marmalade in small bowl. Reserve
½ cup mustard mixture for dipping sauce.

2. Hold 1 pineapple cube and 1 scallop half together. Wrap
with 1 bacon strip. Thread onto skewer. Repeat with remaining
pineapple, scallops and bacon.

3. Place skewers on oiled grid. Grill over medium heat 6 minutes,
turning frequently and brushing with remaining mustard mixture.
Serve hot with reserved dipping sauce.   *Makes 12 skewers*

Tuscan Tuna Crostini

12 thin baguette slices
    Olive oil
1 pouch (4 ounces) STARKIST ALBACORE CREATIONS®,
    Tomato Pesto
2 tablespoons light mayonnaise
2 teaspoons fresh lemon juice
1 small clove garlic, minced

1. Preheat oven to 425°F.

2. Brush bread slices lightly with olive oil. Place on baking sheet.
Bake at 425°F 10 minutes or until lightly toasted.

3. Combine tuna, mayonnaise, lemon juice and garlic.

4. Spread mixture over bread and garnish with fresh basil and
red and yellow pepper strips, if desired.   *Makes 12 servings*

Baked Pork Buns

1 tablespoon vegetable oil
2 cups coarsely chopped bok choy
1 small onion or large shallot, thinly sliced
1 container (18 ounces) refrigerated barbecue shredded pork
2 tablespoons all-purpose flour
2 packages (about 10 ounces each) refrigerated buttermilk
    biscuit dough (5 count each)

1. Preheat oven to 350°F. Grease baking sheet.

2. Heat oil in large skillet over medium-high heat. Add bok choy and onion; cook and stir 8 to 10 minutes or until vegetables are tender. Remove from heat; stir in barbecue pork.

3. Lightly dust clean work surface with flour. Separate biscuit dough into individual biscuits. Working with 1 at a time, split biscuit in half crosswise to create 2 thin biscuits. Roll each biscuit half into 5-inch circle.

4. Spoon heaping tablespoon pork mixture onto one side of each circle. Fold dough over filling to form half circle; press edges to seal. Arrange buns on prepared baking sheet.

5. Bake 12 to 15 minutes or until golden brown.   *Makes 20 buns*

Elegant Appetizer Bites

1 package (8 ounces) cream cheese, softened
2 ounces feta cheese with basil and tomato or plain feta
2 cloves garlic, minced
30 mini phyllo shells (2 (2.1-ounce) packages)
    Prepared toppings such as sundried tomato pesto, basil pesto
      or black olive spread

1. Beat cream cheese, feta and garlic in small bowl with electric mixer at low speed until well blended.

2. Spoon about 1½ teaspoons cheese mixture into each shell. Top with ½ teaspoon desired topping.   *Makes 30 appetizers*

Baked Crab Rangoon

1 can (6 ounces) white crabmeat, drained, flaked
4 ounces (½ of 8-ounce package) PHILADELPHIA® Neufchâtel
    Cheese, ⅓ Less Fat than Cream Cheese, softened
¼ cup thinly sliced green onions
¼ cup KRAFT® Mayo Light Mayonnaise
12 wonton wrappers

PREHEAT oven to 350°F. Mix crabmeat, Neufchâtel cheese, onions and mayo.

SPRAY 12 (2½-inch) muffin cups with cooking spray. Gently place 1 wonton wrapper in each cup, allowing edges of wrappers to extend above sides of cups. Fill evenly with crabmeat mixture.

BAKE 18 to 20 minutes or until edges are golden brown and filling is heated through. Serve warm. Garnish with sliced green onions, if desired.   *Makes 12 servings (1 wonton each)*

Tip: Wonton wrappers are usually found in the grocery store in the refrigerated section of the produce department.

Mini Crab Rangoons: Use 24 wonton wrappers. Gently place 1 wonton wrapper in each of 24 miniature muffin cups sprayed with cooking spray. Fill evenly with crabmeat mixture and bake as directed. Makes 12 servings, 2 wontons each.

Tortilla Roll-Ups

1 (8-ounce) package cream cheese
1 cup chopped black olives
4 green onions, chopped
2 teaspoons Original TABASCO® brand Pepper Sauce
4 to 6 large flour tortillas

Combine cream cheese, olives, green onions and TABASCO® Sauce in medium bowl. Spread thin layer of cream cheese mixture on each tortilla. Starting at one end, gently roll tortilla into tight tube. Wrap with plastic wrap; chill until ready to serve. To serve, unwrap roll, trim edges of tortilla and slice into 8 (1-inch) slices. Serve slices cut sides up.   *Makes 32 to 48 pieces*

Sweet and Spicy Sausage Rounds

   1 pound kielbasa sausage, cut into ¼-inch-thick rounds
   ⅔ cup blackberry jam
   ⅓ cup steak sauce
   1 tablespoon yellow mustard
   ½ teaspoon ground allspice

Slow Cooker Directions

1. Place all ingredients in slow cooker; toss to coat completely. Cover; cook on HIGH 3 hours or until richly glazed.

2. Serve with decorative cocktail picks.   *Makes 6 to 8 servings*

Taco Party Wings

   ¼ cup cornmeal
   1 packet (1.25 ounces) ORTEGA® Taco Seasoning Mix
   2 teaspoons dried parsley flakes
   ¾ teaspoon salt
   2 pounds chicken wing drummettes
   1 bottle (8 ounces) ORTEGA® Taco Sauce

Preheat oven to 350°F.

Mix cornmeal, seasoning mix, parsley and salt together in resealable plastic food storage bag. Add wings, a few at a time, and shake until coated.

Place in single layer on greased shallow baking pans. Generously pour taco sauce onto wings.

Bake 25 minutes. Turn wings over and bake 10 minutes more or until tender. Pour additional taco sauce over wings, if desired.
Makes 12 servings

Note: For spicier wings, try using ORTEGA® Hot Taco Sauce. Serve with blue cheese or ranch dressing for dipping.

Prep Time: 15 minutes • **Start to Finish Time:** 50 minutes

Sesame Chicken Nuggets

1 pound TYSON® Chicken Breast Tenderloins
2 cups corn oil
1 egg, beaten
⅓ cup water
⅓ cup all-purpose flour
1½ tablespoons sesame seeds
1 teaspoon salt

1. Wash hands. Cut chicken into 1×1×½-inch pieces. Add corn oil to deep fryer, filling no more than one-third full. Heat to 375°F. Place egg and water in medium bowl; mix well. Add flour, sesame seeds and salt, stirring until smooth batter is formed. Dip chicken in batter; drain off excess. Wash hands.

2. Add chicken, a few pieces at a time, to hot oil. Fry 4 minutes or until golden brown and internal juices of chicken run clear. (Or insert instant-read meat thermometer into thickest part of chicken. Temperature should read 180°F.) Drain on paper towels. Refrigerate leftovers immediately. *Makes 4 servings*

Serving Suggestion: Serve with your favorite dipping sauces.

Hot Artichoke Dip

1 package (8 ounces) PHILADELPHIA® Cream Cheese, softened
1 can (14 ounces) artichoke hearts, drained, chopped
½ cup KRAFT® Mayo Real Mayonnaise
½ cup KRAFT® 100% Grated Parmesan Cheese
1 clove garlic, minced

MIX all ingredients with electric mixer on medium speed until well blended. Spoon into 9-inch pie plate or quiche dish.

BAKE at 350°F for 20 to 25 minutes or until very lightly browned.

SERVE with NABISCO® Crackers, vegetable dippers or baked pita bread wedges. *Makes 2½ cups*

Special Extras: To make baked pita bread wedges, cut each of 3 split pita breads into 8 triangles. Place on cookie sheet. Bake at 350°F for 10 to 12 minutes or until crisp. Makes 48 wedges.

Caprese-Style Tartlettes

3 tomatoes
3 tablespoons pesto
1 sheet frozen puff pastry (half of 17¼-ounce package), thawed
6 ounces fresh mozzarella cheese
2 tablespoons kalamata olive tapenade (see Note)

1. Cut each tomato into 4 slices (about ⅓ inch thick). Discard tops and bottoms. Place in resealable food storage bag with pesto, turning to coat. Refrigerate 30 minutes or overnight.

2. Preheat oven to 425°F. Line baking sheet with parchment paper.

3. Cut out 6 (4-inch) circles from pastry sheet. Place circles on prepared baking sheet. Top each circle with 2 slices marinated tomato. Bake 12 minutes or until pastry is light golden and puffed.

4. *Turn oven to broil.* Cut mozzarella into 6 (¼-inch-thick) slices. Top each tart with 1 slice mozzarella. Broil 1 minute or until cheese is melted. Top evenly with tapenade. Serve warm.

Makes 6 tartlettes

Note: Tapenade is a Provençal condiment made from minced olives, anchovies, capers, olive oil and seasonings. It's available in large supermarkets and specialty food stores.

BLT Pizza Wedges

12 slices JENNIE-O TURKEY STORE® Turkey Bacon
⅓ cup mayonnaise
4 (6-inch) pre-baked Italian pizza shells
2 Roma tomatoes, thinly sliced
1 cup lettuce, shredded

Heat oven to 450°F. Cook bacon according to package directions. Spread mayonnaise on each pizza shell. Top with sliced tomatoes and bacon. Place on baking sheet. Bake 8 to 10 minutes or until hot. Sprinkle with shredded lettuce. Cut into wedges.

Makes 4 servings

Spicy Peanut-Coconut Shrimp

¼ **cup shredded coconut**
2 **teaspoons dark sesame oil**
1 **pound large raw shrimp, peeled, deveined and patted dry**
¼ **to** ½ **teaspoon red pepper flakes**
2 **tablespoons chopped fresh mint or cilantro (optional)**
¼ **cup chopped lightly salted roasted peanuts**
   Lime wedges (optional)

1. Toast coconut in large nonstick skillet over medium-high heat 2 to 3 minutes or until golden, stirring constantly. Immediately remove from skillet.

2. Heat oil in same skillet over medium-high heat. Add shrimp and red pepper flakes; stir-fry 3 to 4 minutes or until shrimp are pink and opaque. Add mint, if desired; toss well. Top with toasted coconut and chopped peanuts. Garnish with lime wedges.

Makes 4 servings

Serving Suggestion: Serve with steamed sugar snap peas, whole wheat couscous and slices of ripe pineapple.

Dark, or Asian, sesame oil is a strong-flavored, amber-colored oil pressed from toasted sesame seeds. There is also a pale-colored cold-pressed sesame oil which is much lighter in flavor; the two oils are not interchangeable.

Cranberry Chutney Glazed Salmon

½ **teaspoon salt**
½ **teaspoon ground cinnamon**
¼ **teaspoon ground red pepper**
 4 **skinless salmon fillets (5 to 6 ounces each)**
¼ **cup cranberry chutney**
 1 **tablespoon white wine vinegar or cider vinegar**

1. Preheat broiler or prepare grill for indirect cooking. Combine salt, cinnamon and red pepper in small cup; sprinkle over salmon. Combine chutney and vinegar in small bowl; brush evenly over each salmon fillet.

2. Broil 5 to 6 inches from heat source or grill over medium-hot coals on covered grill 4 to 6 minutes or until salmon is opaque in center.   *Makes 4 servings*

Variation: If cranberry chutney is not available, substitute mango chutney. Chop any large pieces of mango.

Broccoli & Noodles Supreme

 3 **cups uncooked medium egg noodles**
 2 **cups broccoli flowerets**
 1 **can (10¾ ounces) CAMPBELL'S® Condensed Cream of**
    Chicken Soup (Regular or 98% Fat Free)
½ **cup sour cream**
⅓ **cup grated Parmesan cheese**
⅛ **teaspoon ground black pepper**

1. Prepare the noodles according to the package directions in a 4-quart saucepot. Add the broccoli during the last 5 minutes of the cooking time. Drain the noodles and broccoli well in a colander and return them to the saucepot.

2. Stir the soup, sour cream, cheese and black pepper into the noodles and broccoli. Cook and stir over medium heat until hot.

3. Top with additional cheese before serving.   *Makes 5 servings*

Prep Time: 10 minutes • **Cook Time:** 20 minutes

Honey Garlic Chicken

2 pounds TYSON® Fresh Chicken Drumsticks
1 cup steak sauce
½ cup honey
1 teaspoon garlic powder
½ teaspoon hot pepper sauce

1. Preheat oven to 375°F. Wash hands. Line bottom of broiler pan with aluminum foil. Place chicken on foil. Wash hands. Combine steak sauce, honey, garlic powder and pepper sauce; pour over chicken.

2. Bake 45 minutes or until internal juices of chicken run clear. (Or insert instant-read meat thermometer into thickest part of chicken. Temperature should read 180°F.) Spoon sauce over chicken. Refrigerate leftovers immediately.   *Makes 8 servings*

Serving Suggestion: Serve with soft breadsticks and a tossed salad.

Prep Time: 5 minutes • **Cook Time:** 45 minutes • **Total Time:** 50 minutes

Quick Mexican Mac

8 ounces elbow macaroni
1 pound ground beef or turkey
1 (1½-ounce) package taco seasoning
1 (28-ounce) can stewed tomatoes
1 (10-ounce) can whole kernel corn, drained
Salt and pepper to taste

Cook pasta according to package directions; drain.

In large skillet over medium heat, brown ground meat until done. Drain fat. Return skillet to burner. Stir taco seasoning into meat. Add tomatoes, corn, salt and pepper. Simmer 3 to 5 minutes or until bubbly.   *Makes 6 servings*

Note: This recipe makes a great quick lunch or six side-dish dinner servings.

*Favorite recipe from **North Dakota Wheat Commission***

Lean Mean Cheeseburger

1 pound ground beef (95% lean)
2 tablespoons quick-cooking oats
½ teaspoon steak seasoning blend
4 seeded *or* whole wheat hamburger buns, split
4 slices lowfat cheese, such as Cheddar *or* American

Toppings:

Lettuce leaves, tomato slices (optional)

1. Place oats in foodsafe plastic bag. Seal bag securely, squeezing out excess air. Roll over bag with rolling pin to crush oats to a fine consistency.

2. Combine ground beef, oats and steak seasoning blend in large bowl, mixing lightly but thoroughly. Lightly shape into four ½-inch patties.

3. Place patties on grid over medium, ash-covered coals. Grill, covered, 11 to 13 minutes (over medium heat on preheated gas grill, covered, 7 to 8 minutes) until instant-read thermometer inserted horizontally into center registers 160°F, turning occasionally.

4. Line bottom of each bun with lettuce and tomato, if desired; top with burger and cheese slice. Close sandwiches.

Makes 4 servings

Tip: Cooking times are for fresh or thoroughly thawed ground beef. Color is not a reliable indicator of ground beef doneness.

Prep and Cook Time: 20 minutes

*Favorite recipe from **Courtesy The Beef Checkoff***

When combining the ingredients for hamburgers, it's important to use a light touch. Mix very briefly and shape the meat into patties gently to avoid burgers that are heavy and dense.

BBQ Chicken Stromboli

1 rotisserie-roasted chicken (2 to 2¼ pounds)
⅓ cup barbecue sauce
1 package (about 13 ounces) refrigerated pizza dough
1 cup (4 ounces) shredded Cheddar cheese
⅓ cup sliced green onions, divided

1. Remove and discard skin from chicken. Shred chicken with forks; discard bones. (You should have about 4 cups shredded chicken.) Combine 2 cups chicken and barbecue sauce in medium bowl until well blended. Cover and refrigerate or freeze remaining chicken for another use.

2. Preheat oven to 400°F. Lightly spray baking sheet with nonstick cooking spray. Unroll pizza dough on baking sheet; pat into 12×9-inch rectangle.

3. Spread chicken mixture lengthwise down center of dough, leaving 2½ inches on each side. Sprinkle with Cheddar and ¼ cup green onions. Fold long sides of dough over filling; press edges to seal.

4. Sprinkle with remaining green onions. Bake 19 to 22 minutes or until golden brown. Let stand 10 minutes before slicing.

Makes 6 servings

Belgioioso® Fresh Mozzarella Pizza

Dough for 2 (13-inch) pizzas
3 tablespoons olive oil
4 ripe plum tomatoes, cut into thin slices
2 cups (10 ounces) diced BELGIOIOSO® Fresh Mozzarella
½ teaspoon salt
12 fresh basil leaves

Preheat oven to 425°F. Place pizza dough on lightly oiled pans. Brush each with 1 tablespoon olive oil. Place tomato slices on dough; sprinkle cheese, salt and remaining olive oil on top. Bake pizzas for 25 to 30 minutes or until crusts are nicely browned. Top with basil. Cut into wedges and serve.

Makes 4 servings

Super Fast Suppers

Cheddar-Swiss Strata

Vegetable cooking spray
6 cups French or Italian bread, cut in cubes
1 can (10¾ ounces) CAMPBELL'S® Condensed Cheddar Cheese
   Soup
4 eggs, beaten
1 cup milk
1½ cups shredded Swiss cheese (6 ounces)

1. Spray a 12×8×2-inch shallow baking dish with cooking spray. Put the bread in the dish.

2. Beat the soup, eggs, milk and cheese with a whisk in a medium bowl. Pour the soup mixture over the bread. Cover and refrigerate overnight.

3. Uncover the dish. Bake at 350°F for 40 minutes or until a knife inserted near the center comes out clean. Let the strata stand for 10 minutes before serving. *Makes 6 servings*

Cooking for a Crowd Tip: Recipe may be doubled. Double all ingredients. Divide the ingredients evenly between 2 greased (12×8×2-inch) shallow baking dishes.

Zesty One-Skillet Sausage Dish

1 pound hot Italian turkey sausage, cut into 1-inch pieces
2 cans (15 ounces each) whole kernel corn, drained
1 cup prepared thick chunky salsa (medium to hot)
½ cup black olives, pitted and sliced
1 cup shredded mozzarella cheese
Corn tortillas

1. In large skillet, over medium heat, cook sausage, corn and salsa. Cover and simmer over low heat 10 to 15 minutes or until sausage is no longer pink in center.

2. Stir in olives. Remove from heat.

3. Stir in cheese, cover and let stand until cheese is melted. Serve with corn tortillas. *Makes 4 servings*

*Favorite recipe from **National Turkey Federation***

Spinach & Roasted Pepper Panini

1 loaf (12 ounces) focaccia
1½ cups spinach leaves (about 12 leaves)
1 jar (about 7 ounces) roasted red peppers, drained
4 ounces fontina cheese, thinly sliced
¾ cup thinly sliced red onion
1 tablespoon olive oil

1. Cut focaccia in half horizontally. Layer bottom half with spinach, peppers, fontina and onion. Cover with top half of focaccia. Brush outsides of sandwich with oil. Cut sandwich into 4 equal pieces.

2. Heat large nonstick skillet over medium heat. Add sandwiches; press down lightly with spatula or weigh down with plate. Cook sandwiches 4 to 5 minutes per side or until cheese melts and sandwiches are golden brown.   *Makes 4 servings*

Pepper Steak

1½ pounds flank steak, cut crosswise into thin strips
1 cup plus 2 tablespoons MRS. DASH® Spicy Teriyaki
    10-Minute Marinade, divided
1 tablespoon vegetable oil
2 medium green bell peppers, seeded and sliced
2 medium red bell peppers, seeded and sliced
1 large onion, halved and cut crosswise into thin slices

1. Marinate flank steak in 1 cup of MRS. DASH® Spicy Teriyaki 10-Minute Marinade for at least 10 minutes. Remove steak and discard marinade.

2. Heat oil in a 12-inch skillet. Add flank steak and cook until browned, about 4 minutes.

3. Transfer steak to a bowl and cover. Add peppers, onion and remaining 2 tablespoons MRS. DASH® Spicy Teriyaki 10-Minute Marinade to skillet. Cook until onion is golden brown and peppers are crisp-tender, about 6 minutes.

4. Return steak to skillet and cook with pepper mixture on high heat about 3 minutes or until cooked through.   *Makes 6 servings*

Chorizo and Papa Burritos

14 ounces Mexican-style chorizo
2 small russet potatoes, peeled and diced (about 6 ounces)
8 taco-size flour tortillas
½ cup (2 ounces) shredded Monterey Jack cheese
¼ cup sour cream

1. Remove and discard casing from chorizo. Heat medium skillet over medium heat. Crumble chorizo into skillet; brown 6 to 8 minutes, stirring to separate meat. Add potatoes; cook and stir about 12 minutes or until potatoes are tender. Drain fat.

2. To heat tortillas on gas stove, place tortilla directly on burner over low flame; turn with tongs when tortilla begins to brown, about 10 seconds. Heat until browned on both sides. To heat on electric range, preheat burner 2 minutes on medium heat. Place tortilla directly on burner; turn with tongs when tortilla begins to brown, about 10 seconds. Heat until browned on both sides.

3. Spoon about ¼ cup chorizo mixture in center of each tortilla; top with 1 tablespoon cheese and 1½ teaspoons sour cream. Fold bottom of tortillas up over bottom third of filling. Fold in sides of tortillas over filling. *Makes 8 mini burritos*

Note: If using 4 fajita-size flour tortillas, use ½ cup filling per tortilla.

Cheesy Tuna Veg•All® Casserole

3 cups cooked noodles
2 cans (15 ounces each) VEG•ALL® Original Mixed Vegetables, drained
1 can (10¾ ounces) cream of mushroom soup
1 can (9 ounces) tuna, drained
1 cup grated Cheddar cheese

Preheat oven to 350°F. Combine all ingredients in a 1½- to 2-quart casserole; blend well. Bake 30 minutes or until heated through. *Makes 4 to 6 servings*

Skillet Chicken with Olives

4 **TYSON® Trimmed & Ready™ Fresh Boneless Skinless Chicken Breasts**
2 **teaspoons garlic salt**
2 **tablespoons olive oil**
⅓ **cup pitted black olives**
¼ **cup lemon juice**
1 **teaspoon dried basil**

1. Wash hands. Sprinkle chicken with garlic salt. Heat oil in large nonstick skillet over medium-high heat. Cook chicken 4 to 6 minutes or until golden brown on both sides.

2. Reduce heat to medium-low. Add olives, lemon juice and basil to skillet. Cover and cook 8 minutes longer or until internal juices of chicken run clear. (Or insert instant-read meat thermometer into thickest part of chicken. Temperature should read 180°F.) Refrigerate leftovers immediately. *Makes 4 servings*

Serving Suggestion: Serve with steamed green beans and spaghetti with pesto.

Cook Time: 15 minutes • **Total Time:** 15 minutes

Crunchy Cajun Fish Fingers

2⅔ **cups** *French's®* **French Fried Onions**
2 **teaspoons Cajun spice blend**
2 **tablespoons reduced-fat mayonnaise**
1 **teaspoon** *Frank's® RedHot®* **Original Cayenne Pepper Sauce**
1 **pound catfish or tilapia fillets, cut crosswise into 1-inch strips**

1. Mix French Fried Onions and Cajun spice in plastic bag. Crush with hands or rolling pin.

2. Combine mayonnaise and *Frank's RedHot* Sauce in large bowl. Add fish strips to bowl and toss to coat. Add fish strips to onion crumbs, pressing firmly to adhere.

3. Bake fish strips on foil-lined baking sheet at 400°F for 15 minutes or until fish flakes with a fork. *Makes 4 servings*

Prep Time: 10 minutes • **Cook Time:** 15 minutes

Grilled Steak with Arugula & Gorgonzola Salad

4 boneless beef top loin (strip) steaks (¾ inch thick)
1 cup balsamic or red wine vinaigrette, divided
2 cups mixed salad greens
1½ cups baby arugula leaves
½ cup crumbled Gorgonzola cheese

1. Combine steaks and ½ cup vinaigrette in large resealable food storage bag. Seal bag; turn to coat. Marinate in refrigerator 20 to 30 minutes. Meanwhile, prepare grill for direct cooking.

2. Remove steaks from marinade; discard marinade. Grill steaks over medium-high heat, covered, 6 to 8 minutes for medium rare (145°F) or until desired doneness, turning once.

3. Meanwhile, combine salad greens and arugula in medium bowl. Pour remaining ½ cup vinaigrette over greens; toss until well coated. Serve steaks with salad. Sprinkle with gorgonzola.

Makes 4 servings

Potato Skillet Toss

2 tablespoons vegetable oil, divided
1½ cups chopped onions
8 ounces andouille sausage, diced
1 red or green bell pepper, diced
½ teaspoon dried oregano
1 package (20 ounces) refrigerated diced potatoes
¼ teaspoon salt

1. Heat 1 tablespoon oil in large skillet over medium-high heat. Add onions; cook and stir 6 minutes or until translucent. Add sausage, bell pepper and oregano; cook and stir 2 minutes. Push mixture to side of skillet.

2. Heat remaining 1 tablespoon oil in skillet over medium heat. Add potatoes; cook according to package directions. (Reduce heat slightly if potatoes brown too quickly.) Sprinkle with salt.

Makes 5 servings

Polska Kielbasa with Beer & Onions

    18 ounces brown ale or beer
    ⅓ cup packed dark brown sugar
    ⅓ cup honey mustard
    2 kielbasa sausages (16 ounces each), cut into 4-inch pieces
    2 onions, quartered

Slow Cooker Directions

1. Combine ale, brown sugar and honey mustard in slow cooker. Add sausage pieces; top with onions.

2. Cover; cook on LOW 4 to 5 hours, stirring occasionally.

Makes 6 to 8 servings

Quick Skillet Chicken & Macaroni Parmesan

    1 jar (1 pound 10 ounces) PREGO® Traditional Italian Sauce
    ¼ cup grated Parmesan cheese
    3 cups cubed cooked chicken
    1½ cups elbow macaroni, cooked and drained
    1½ cups shredded part-skim mozzarella cheese (6 ounces)

1. Heat the Italian sauce, **3 tablespoons** of the Parmesan cheese, chicken and macaroni in a 10-inch skillet over medium-high heat to a boil. Reduce the heat to medium. Cover and cook for 10 minutes or until the mixture is hot and bubbling, stirring occasionally.

2. Sprinkle with the mozzarella cheese and remaining Parmesan cheese. Let stand for 5 minutes or until the cheese melts.

Makes 6 servings

Kitchen Tip: Use 1½ pounds skinless, boneless chicken breasts, cut into cubes for the cooked chicken. Heat 1 tablespoon olive oil in a 12-inch skillet over medium-high heat. Add the chicken in 2 batches and cook until it's well browned, stirring often. Continue to cook, proceeding as directed in step 1 above.

Sun-Dried Tomato Risotto

1 jar (8 ounces) oil-packed sun-dried tomatoes
1½ cups uncooked Arborio rice or regular long-grain white rice
4 cups SWANSON® Chicken Broth (Regular, Natural Goodness®
or Certified Organic), heated
1 cup frozen peas, thawed
¼ cup walnuts, toasted and chopped

1. Drain the tomatoes, reserving **2 tablespoons** oil. Chop enough tomatoes to make ½ **cup**.

2. Heat the reserved oil in a 3-quart saucepan over medium heat. Add the tomatoes and rice and cook and stir for 2 minutes.

3. Add **1 cup** broth and cook and stir until it's absorbed. Add the remaining broth, ½ **cup** at a time, stirring until it's absorbed before adding more. Stir in the peas and walnuts with the last broth addition.

4. Remove the saucepan from the heat. Cover and let stand for 5 minutes. *Makes 4 servings*

Kitchen Tip: To quickly thaw the peas, place them in a colander and run under warm water.

Parmesan Sun-Dried Tomato Risotto: Substitute grated Parmesan cheese for the walnuts.

Prep Time: 5 minutes • **Cook Time:** 25 minutes • **Stand Time:** 5 minutes

Green Beans with Maple-Bacon Dressing

½ **cup chicken broth**
1 **package (16 ounces) frozen French-style green beans**
2 **tablespoons bacon bits**
2 **tablespoons maple syrup**
2 **tablespoons cider vinegar**
¼ **teaspoon black pepper**

1. Bring broth to a boil in large saucepan. Add beans; cover and simmer over medium heat about 7 minutes or until beans are crisp-tender. Drain; place beans in serving bowl.

2. Combine bacon bits, syrup, vinegar and pepper in small bowl. Pour over beans; toss to coat. *Makes 6 servings*

Homestead Succotash

¼ **pound bacon, diced**
1 **cup chopped onion**
½ **teaspoon dried thyme leaves**
1 **can (15¼ ounces) DEL MONTE® Whole Kernel Golden Sweet Corn, drained**
1 **can (15¼ ounces) DEL MONTE Green Lima Beans, drained**

1. Cook bacon in skillet until crisp; drain. Add onion and thyme; cook until onion is tender.

2. Stir in vegetables and heat through. *Makes 6 to 8 servings*

Microwave Directions: In shallow 1-quart microwavable dish, cook bacon on HIGH 6 minutes or until crisp; drain. Add onion and thyme; cover and cook on HIGH 2 to 3 minutes or until onion is tender. Add vegetables. Cover and cook on HIGH 3 to 4 minutes or until heated through.

Prep and Cook Time: 13 minutes

Creamy Baked Carrots

Vegetable cooking spray
1 can (10¾ ounces) CAMBPBELL'S® Condensed Cream of Celery Soup (Regular or 98% Fat Free)
½ cup milk
½ teaspoon dried thyme leaves, crushed
1 bag (20 ounces) frozen crinkle-cut carrots, thawed (about 5 cups)
1 can (2.8 ounces) French fried onions (1⅓ cups)

1. Spray a 2-quart casserole with cooking spray. Stir the soup, milk, thyme, carrots and ⅔ **cup** of the onions in the prepared dish.

2. Bake at 350°F for 35 minutes. Stir the carrot mixture.

3. Sprinkle the remaining onions over the carrot mixture. Bake for 5 minutes more or until carrots are tender and onions are golden brown.   *Makes 6 servings*

Prep Time: 5 minutes • **Bake Time:** 40 minutes

Spanish-Style Rice

1 tablespoon vegetable oil
1 cup uncooked regular long-grain white rice
4 cups V8® 100% Vegetable Juice (Regular or Low Sodium)
1 teaspoon dried basil leaves, crushed
¼ teaspoon garlic powder
2 cups frozen mixed vegetables

1. Heat the oil in a 10-inch skillet over medium heat. Add the rice and cook for 30 seconds, stirring constantly.

2. Stir the vegetable juice, basil and garlic powder in the skillet and heat to a boil. Reduce the heat to low. Cover and cook for 15 minutes.

3. Stir in the vegetables. Cover and cook for 10 minutes or until the rice and vegetables are tender.   *Makes 4 servings*

Kitchen Tip: This recipe is delicious as a side dish or wrapped with chicken and cheese in a burrito.

Prep Time: 5 minutes • **Cook Time:** 30 minutes

Mexican Mashed Potatoes

3 pounds russet potatoes, peeled and diced
4 tablespoons (½ stick) butter
¼ cup milk
1 can (4 ounces) ORTEGA® Fire-Roasted Diced Green Chiles
   Salt, to taste
   Black pepper, to taste
1 packet (1.25 ounces) ORTEGA® Taco Seasoning Mix

Bring large saucepot of salted water to a boil. Add potatoes. Cook 10 minutes or until soft. Drain water from pot.

Add butter, milk, chiles, salt and pepper to taste. Mash well. Stir in seasoning mix. Serve warm.   *Makes 6 servings*

Tip: For an even richer side dish, stir in 1 cup shredded Cheddar or Monterey Jack cheese.

Prep Time: 5 minutes • **Start to Finish Time:** 25 minutes

Cauliflower with Creamy Dijon Sauce

1 small head cauliflower (1¾ pounds), trimmed and cut into
   florets (4 cups)
2 tablespoons water
3 tablespoons sour cream
2 tablespoons Dijon mustard
¼ cup panko bread crumbs*
¼ cup grated Asiago or Parmesan cheese

Or substitute ¼ cup fresh whole grain bread crumbs, toasted in a 400°F oven or toaster oven 3 to 4 minutes or until golden brown.

Microwave Directions

Place cauliflower and water in microwavable casserole. Cover and microwave on HIGH 5 to 6 minutes or until tender. Drain and return to casserole. Add sour cream and mustard; toss to coat. Sprinkle with bread crumbs and Asiago.   *Makes 4 servings*

Sesame-Honey Vegetable Casserole

1 package (16 ounces) frozen mixed vegetable medley, such as baby carrots, broccoli, onions and red bell peppers, thawed and drained
3 tablespoons honey
1 tablespoon dark sesame oil
1 tablespoon soy sauce
2 teaspoons sesame seeds

1. Preheat oven to 350°F. Place vegetables in shallow 1½-quart casserole.

2. Combine honey, sesame oil, soy sauce and sesame seeds in small bowl; stir until well blended. Drizzle evenly over vegetables. Bake 20 to 25 minutes or until vegetables are tender and hot, stirring after 15 minutes.   *Makes 4 servings*

Simple Snow Peas & Mushroom Salad

½ cup WISH-BONE® Italian or Light Italian Dressing
1 package (8 ounces) snow peas, trimmed
1 cup sliced mushrooms
1 medium red bell pepper, cut into strips
1 package (5 ounces) mixed salad greens

Combine all ingredients except salad greens in large bowl. Cover and marinate in refrigerator, stirring occasionally, at least 30 minutes.

Arrange salad greens on serving platter, then top with marinated vegetables.   *Makes 5 servings*

Prep Time: 15 minutes • **Marinate Time:** 30 minutes

Sweet Potatoes with Cranberry-Ginger Glaze

   2 medium sweet potatoes
   ½ cup dried cranberries
   ¼ cup cranberry juice
   ¼ cup maple syrup
   2 slices (⅛ inch thick) fresh ginger
   Dash black pepper

1. Pierce potatoes all over with fork. Microwave on HIGH 10 minutes or until soft. Peel and cut potatoes into wedges; place in serving dish.

2. Meanwhile, for glaze, combine cranberries, juice, syrup, ginger and pepper in small saucepan. Cook over low heat 7 to 10 minutes or until syrupy. Discard ginger. Pour glaze over potatoes.   *Makes 4 servings*

Creole Creamed Spinach

   3 slices thick-cut bacon, diced
   1 cup chopped onion
   2 packages (10 ounces each) frozen chopped spinach,
       thawed and squeezed dry
 1¼ cups half-and-half or whipping cream
   1 teaspoon Creole or Cajun seasoning*

*Creole or Cajun seasoning is usually a blend of garlic, black pepper, ground red pepper, oregano, chili pepper, salt, onion, paprika and red and green bell peppers. It can be found in the spice section of most supermarkets.

1. Cook bacon in large skillet over medium heat until crisp; drain on paper towel.

2. Cook and stir onion in drippings about 6 minutes or until tender. Add spinach, half-and-half and seasoning; mix well. Simmer 2 minutes. Transfer to serving dish. Sprinkle with bacon.
                         Makes 6 servings

Rice and Cranberry Pilaf

1 cup chicken broth
1 cup white cranberry juice
2 cups MINUTE® White Rice, uncooked
¼ cup dried cranberries
¼ cup almonds, sliced, toasted
1 teaspoon orange peel, grated (optional)

Pour broth and cranberry juice into medium saucepan. Bring to a boil over medium-high heat.

Stir in rice and cranberries; return to a boil. Cover; remove from heat. Let stand 5 minutes. Stir in almonds. Top with orange peel, if desired. *Makes 6 servings*

Tip: To toast almonds quickly, spread them in a single layer in heavy-bottomed skillet. Cook over medium heat 1 to 2 minutes, stirring frequently, until nuts are lightly browned. Remove from skillet immediately. Cool before using.

Herb Focaccia

1 loaf (1 pound) frozen bread dough
2 tablespoons olive oil
1 to 2 tablespoons fresh rosemary, sage or other herbs
1 clove garlic, finely chopped
1 teaspoon chicken-flavor instant bouillon
3 tablespoons grated Parmesan cheese

Thaw dough according to package directions. Roll dough into 12×8-inch rectangle. Place on baking sheet coated with nonstick cooking spray. Cover and let stand 15 minutes. Combine oil, herbs, garlic and bouillon in small skillet; simmer 5 minutes or until bouillon dissolves.

Dimple dough vigorously with fingertips. Brush with herb mixture. Bake on lowest rack of preheated 450°F oven for 10 minutes; sprinkle with cheese and bake 5 to 10 minutes or until bottom is browned. Cut into squares. *Makes 12 servings*

Favorite recipe from **North Dakota Wheat Commission**

Lemon Herb Broccoli Casserole

1 can (10¾ ounces) CAMPBELL'S® Condensed Cream of
    Chicken with Herbs Soup
½ cup milk
1 tablespoon lemon juice
1 bag (16 ounces) frozen broccoli cuts, thawed (about 4 cups)
1 can (2.8 ounces) French fried onions (1⅓ cups)

1. Stir the soup, milk, lemon juice, broccoli and ⅔ **cup** onions in
a 1½-quart casserole and cover.

2. Bake at 350°F for 25 minutes or until the broccoli is tender.
Stir the broccoli mixture.

3. Sprinkle the remaining onions over the broccoli mixture. Bake
for 5 minutes more or until the onions are golden brown.

Makes 6 servings

Time-Saving Tip: To thaw the broccoli, cut off one corner of bag
and microwave on HIGH for 5 minutes.

Prep Time: 10 minutes • **Bake Time:** 30 minutes

Mozzarella Zucchini Skillet

2 tablespoons vegetable oil
5 medium zucchini, sliced (about 7½ cups)
1 medium onion, chopped (about ½ cup)
¼ teaspoon garlic powder or 2 cloves garlic, minced
1½ cups PREGO® Traditional Italian Sauce
½ cup shredded mozzarella or Cheddar cheese

1. Heat the oil in a 12-inch skillet over medium-high heat. Add the
zucchini, onion and garlic powder and cook until the vegetables
are tender-crisp.

2. Stir in the sauce and heat through.

3. Sprinkle with the cheese. Cover and cook until the cheese
melts.

Makes 7 servings

Prep Time: 10 minutes • **Cook Time:** 15 minutes

Pesto Rice Salad

2 cups MINUTE® White Rice, uncooked
1 package (7 ounces) basil pesto sauce
1 cup cherry tomatoes, halved
8 ounces whole-milk mozzarella cheese, cut into ½-inch cubes
⅓ cup Parmesan cheese, shredded
 Toasted pine nuts (optional)

Prepare rice according to package directions. Place in large bowl. Let stand 10 minutes.

Add pesto sauce; mix well. Gently stir in tomatoes and cheese.

Serve warm or cover and refrigerate until ready to serve. Sprinkle with pine nuts, if desired. *Makes 6 servings*

Tip: To toast pine nuts, spread in single layer in heavy-bottomed skillet. Cook over medium heat 1 to 2 minutes, stirring frequently, until nuts are lightly browned. Remove from skillet immediately. Cool before using.

Tip: For a heartier meal, add 1 package (6 ounces) grilled chicken breast strips to the prepared salad.

Asian Vegetables and Ham

2 cups reduced-sodium chicken broth
1 pound frozen stir-fry vegetables
1 teaspoon sesame oil
4 ounces thinly sliced ham, cut into ½-inch squares
2 cups uncooked instant white long grain rice
 Soy sauce (optional)

Place broth, vegetables and sesame oil in large saucepan; bring to a boil over high heat. Remove from heat; stir in ham and rice. Cover and let stand 5 minutes. Serve with soy sauce, if desired.
Makes 4 servings

Variation: Substitute 12 ounces cooked chicken for the ham.

Pepperminty Ice Cream Sandwiches

1 package (about 18 ounces) devil's food cake mix
5 tablespoons butter, melted
3 eggs
50 hard peppermint candies, unwrapped
1 quart vanilla ice cream

1. Preheat oven to 350°F. Spray cookie sheets lightly with nonstick cooking spray.

2. Beat cake mix, butter and eggs in large bowl with electric mixer at medium speed 1 to 2 minutes or until blended and smooth. Drop dough by rounded tablespoonfuls 2 inches apart on prepared cookie sheets.

3. Bake 12 minutes or until edges are set and centers are no longer shiny. Cool 5 minutes on cookie sheets. Remove to wire racks; cool completely.

4. Place peppermint candies in medium resealable food storage bag. Seal bag; crush candies with rolling pin or back of small skillet. Place crushed candies in small bowl. Line shallow baking pan with waxed paper.

5. Place scoop of ice cream on flat side of 1 cookie. Top with second cookie; roll edge in crushed candies. Place on prepared pan. Repeat with remaining ice cream, cookies and candies. Cover pan and freeze until ready to serve.

Makes about 1½ dozen sandwiches

Pastry Twists

**½ of a 17.3 ounce package PEPPERIDGE FARM® Frozen
  Puff Pastry Sheets (1 sheet)**
 1 egg, beaten
   Generous dash salt
⅔ cup pecan halves, finely chopped
½ cup sugar
½ teaspoon ground cinnamon

1. Thaw the pastry sheet at room temperature for 40 minutes or until it is easy to handle. Line a 15×10-inch jelly roll pan with parchment paper or aluminum foil. Stir the egg and salt with a fork in a small bowl.

2. Unfold the pastry on a lightly floured surface. Roll the sheet into a 12-inch square. Brush pastry with the egg mixture.

3. Mix the pecans, sugar and cinnamon in a small bowl. Sprinkle the nut mixture over half of the pastry. Fold the other pastry half over the nut filling. Slide onto a pan and refrigerate 30 minutes or until the pastry is firm.

4. Roll the pastry on a lightly floured surface into a 12-inch square. Use a pizza cutter to cut the dough crosswise into 24 (½-inch-wide) strips. Twist the top of each strip in one direction and the bottom in the opposite direction several times to form a corkscrew shape. Place each twist 2 inches apart across the width (10-inch side) of the prepared pan. Press the ends of each twist against the sides of the pan so they stick. (This keeps the twists from unraveling while they are baking.) Refrigerate for 1 hour.

5. Heat oven to 350°F. Bake for 20 minutes or until golden and well caramelized. Cool in pan on a wire rack for 5 minutes. While the twists are still flexible and before they cool completely, trim the ends with a sharp knife. If you wish, cut the twists in half. Serve with a creamy dessert or as a tea pastry. Store twists between sheets of waxed paper in an airtight container.   *Makes 24 twists*

Cinnamon-Sugar Twists: Mix 2 tablespoons sugar and 1 teaspoon ground cinnamon.

Choco-Berry Twists: Spread pastry with 2 tablespoons seedless raspberry jam and sprinkle with ⅓ cup mini semi-sweet chocolate pieces.

Chocolate Stuffed Doughnuts

½ **cup semisweet chocolate chips**
2 **tablespoons whipping cream**
1 **package (7½ ounces) refrigerated buttermilk biscuit dough
     (10 count)**
½ **cup granulated or powdered sugar**
¾ **cup vegetable oil**

1. Combine chocolate chips and cream in small microwavable bowl. Microwave on HIGH 20 seconds; stir until smooth. Cover and refrigerate 1 hour or until solid.

2. Separate dough into individual biscuits. Using melon baller or small teaspoon, scoop out 1 rounded teaspoon chocolate mixture; place in center of each biscuit. Press dough around chocolate and pinch to form a ball. Roll pinched end on work surface to seal dough and flatten ball slightly.

3. Place sugar in shallow dish; set aside. Heat oil in small skillet until hot but not smoking. Cook doughnuts in small batches about 30 seconds per side or until golden brown on both sides. Drain on paper towels.

4. Roll warm doughnuts in sugar to coat. Serve warm or at room temperature. (Doughnuts are best within a few hours of cooking.)
Makes 10 doughnuts

Tip: For a quicker chocolate filling, use chocolate chips instead of the chocolate-cream mixture. Place 6 to 8 chips in the center of each biscuit; proceed with shaping and cooking doughnuts as directed.

Frozen Lemonade Squares

9 HONEY MAID® Low Fat Honey Grahams, finely crushed
(about 1¼ cups crumbs)
⅓ cup margarine or butter, melted
1 quart (4 cups) frozen vanilla yogurt, softened
1 can (6 ounces) frozen lemonade concentrate, thawed
½ cup thawed COOL WHIP LITE® Whipped Topping
Fresh mint sprigs and lemon slices (optional)

MIX graham crumbs and margarine. Press firmly onto bottom of 9-inch square pan.

BEAT yogurt and lemonade concentrate in large bowl with electric mixer on medium speed until well blended. Spread over crust.

FREEZE 4 hours or until firm. Cut into squares. Top each square with a dollop of whipped topping. Garnish with fresh mint sprigs and lemon slices, if desired.   *Makes 9 servings (1 square each)*

Jazz It Up: Serve this refreshing dessert with fresh raspberries.

Strawberry Sundae Pie

¼ cup creamy peanut butter
3 tablespoons light corn syrup
2 cups crisp rice cereal
1¾ cups chocolate frozen yogurt, slightly softened
1½ cups strawberry or raspberry sorbet
Sliced strawberries (optional)

1. Spray 9-inch pie plate with nonstick cooking spray. Combine peanut butter and corn syrup in medium bowl; stir until blended. Stir in cereal until coated. Press onto bottom and up side of prepared pie plate. Loosely cover and refrigerate 15 minutes.

2. Gently spread frozen yogurt over crust. Use small ice cream scoop to scoop sorbet into small balls; arrange over yogurt layer. Cover and freeze about 2 hours or until firm.

3. Let pie stand at room temperature 10 minutes. Cut into wedges; garnish with sliced strawberries.   *Makes 8 servings*

Peanut Butter Cookie Bars

1 package (16 ounces) refrigerated peanut butter cookie
   dough
1 can (14 ounces) sweetened condensed milk
¼ cup all-purpose flour
¼ cup peanut butter
1 cup peanut butter chips and/or chopped peanuts

1. Preheat oven to 350°F. Lightly grease 13×9-inch baking pan. Let dough stand at room temperature about 15 minutes.

2. Press dough evenly onto bottom of prepared pan. Bake 10 minutes.

3. Meanwhile, combine sweetened condensed milk, flour and peanut butter in medium bowl; beat until well blended. Spread over partially baked crust. Sprinkle evenly with peanut butter chips; press down lightly.

4. Bake 15 to 18 minutes or until center is set. Cool completely in pan on wire rack.   *Makes about 2 dozen bars*

Grilled Banana & Chocolate Panini

¼ cup (½ stick) butter, softened
1 frozen pound cake (about 10 ounces), thawed, cut into
   12 (½-inch-thick) slices
1 cup chocolate hazelnut spread
3 ripe bananas, cut lengthwise into slices
¼ teaspoon ground cinnamon

1. Lightly butter one side of each pound cake slice.

2. For each panini, lay 1 slice pound cake, buttered side down, on work surface. Spread with about 1 tablespoon chocolate hazelnut spread; top with banana slices and sprinkle with cinnamon. Top with second slice pound cake, buttered side up.

3. Spray indoor grill with nonstick cooking spray; heat to medium. Cook about 2 minutes or until pound cake is golden brown.
                    Makes 6 servings

Warm Chocolate Risotto

1 cup MINUTE® White Rice, uncooked
1 cup milk
⅓ cup sugar
½ cup semisweet chocolate chips
¼ cup heavy cream
2 tablespoons unsalted butter
Fresh mint leaves (optional)

Combine rice, milk and sugar in medium saucepan. Bring to a boil. Remove from heat, cover and let stand 5 minutes.

Stir in chocolate chips, cream and butter until melted. Garnish with mint leaves, if desired. *Makes 4 servings*

Creamy Lemon Pie

3 egg yolks
1 (14-ounce) can EAGLE BRAND® Sweetened Condensed Milk (NOT evaporated milk)
½ cup lemon juice
1 (8- or 9-inch) prepared graham cracker or baked pie crust
Whipped topping or whipped cream
Lemon curl or grated lemon rind

1. Preheat oven to 325°F.

2. Beat egg yolks in medium bowl; gradually beat in EAGLE BRAND® and lemon juice. Pour into crust.

3. Bake 30 to 35 minutes or until set. Remove from oven. Cool 1 hour. Chill at least 3 hours.

4. Before serving, spread whipped topping over pie. Garnish with lemon curl or rind. Store leftovers covered in refrigerator.
Makes one (8- or 9-inch) pie

Note: To make a lemon curl, cut a strip of lemon rind—yellow part only—using a paring knife or zester. Wind around a straw or chopstick, and secure with plastic wrap. Let stand 1 hour. To use, unwrap, slide the curl off the straw, and arrange attractively on pie.

Chocolate Cheesecakes for Two

2 ounces (¼ of 8-ounce package) PHILADELPHIA® Cream Cheese, softened
1 tablespoon sugar
1 square BAKER'S® Semi-Sweet Baking Chocolate, melted
½ cup thawed COOL WHIP® Whipped Topping
2 OREO® Chocolate Sandwich Cookies

BEAT cream cheese, sugar and chocolate in medium bowl with wire whisk until well blended. Add whipped topping; mix well.

PLACE 1 cookie on bottom of each of 2 paper-lined medium muffin cups; fill evenly with cream cheese mixture.

REFRIGERATE 2 hours or overnight. (Or, if you are in a hurry, place in the freezer for 1 hour.) *Makes 2 servings*

Jazz It Up: Dust surface with cocoa powder. Top with heart-shaped stencil; dust with powdered sugar.

S'more Brownies

1 package (about 19 ounces) brownie mix
2 eggs
½ cup vegetable oil
¼ cup water
1 jar (7½ ounces) marshmallow creme
12 graham crackers

1. Preheat oven to 350°F. Spray 13×9-inch baking pan with nonstick cooking spray.

2. Combine brownie mix, eggs, oil and water in large bowl; mix well. Pour into prepared pan. Bake 25 minutes or until set in center. Cool in pan 10 minutes. Spread marshmallow creme evenly over brownie. Let stand 5 minutes.

3. Break graham crackers in half to form squares. Arrange layer of crackers over marshmallow layer. Cut around each square; carefully remove brownies from pan. Place 1 graham cracker square under each brownie; press to adhere. Let brownies cool to room temperature before serving. *Makes 12 brownies*

Fruity Oatmeal Jumbles

1 package (16 ounces) refrigerated oatmeal raisin cookie
    dough
3 tablespoons all-purpose flour
1 egg white
1 cup dried fruit bits
½ cup shelled pistachio nuts

1. Preheat oven to 350°F. Lightly grease cookie sheets. Let dough stand at room temperature 15 minutes.

2. Combine dough, flour and egg white in large bowl; beat until well blended. Stir in fruit bits and pistachios. (Dough will be very sticky.) Drop dough by heaping tablespoonfuls 2 inches apart onto prepared cookie sheets.

3. Bake about 15 minutes or until edges are browned. Cool on cookie sheets 2 minutes. Remove to wire racks; cool completely.

Makes 1½ dozen cookies

Blackberry Panna Cotta

3 cups frozen unsweetened blackberries, thawed
2 cups whipping cream
1 cup buttermilk
¾ cup sugar
3 tablespoons water
1 envelope (¼ ounce) unflavored gelatin

1. Process blackberries in food processor or blender until smooth. Combine cream, buttermilk and sugar in medium saucepan over medium heat. Add blackberry purée; bring to a simmer over low heat.

2. Pour water into small saucepan; sprinkle with gelatin. Heat over low heat, swirling pan until gelatin is dissolved. Add to blackberry mixture; stir until combined.

3. Strain mixture through fine mesh sieve or strainer, pressing down with rubber spatula. Pour evenly into 6 (8-ounce) ramekins or custard cups. Refrigerate 6 hours or until set. To serve, invert and unmold onto serving plates.

Makes 6 servings

Easy Chocolate Truffles

  1 package (8 ounces) PHILADELPHIA® Cream Cheese, softened
  3 cups powdered sugar
1½ packages (12 squares) BAKER'S® Semi-Sweet Baking
      Chocolate, melted
1½ teaspoons vanilla
    Suggested coatings: ground PLANTERS® Walnuts, unsweetened
      cocoa, powdered sugar and/or BAKER'S ANGEL FLAKE®
      Coconut

BEAT cream cheese in large bowl with electric mixer on medium speed until smooth. Gradually add sugar, mixing until well blended.

ADD melted chocolate and vanilla; mix well. Refrigerate 1 hour or until chilled.

SHAPE into 1-inch balls. Roll in walnuts, cocoa, powdered sugar or coconut. Store in refrigerator.   *Makes 24 servings (3 truffles each)*

Easy Spirited Chocolate Truffles: Prepare as directed except omit vanilla. Divide truffle mixture into thirds. Add 1 tablespoon liqueur (almond, coffee or orange-flavored) to each third of mixture; mix well.

Pomegranate-Glazed Pears

4 firm ripe Bosc pears
1 cup pomegranate, blueberry or cranberry-cherry juice
1 to 2 tablespoons honey, or to taste
¼ teaspoon ground cinnamon
½ cup crushed biscotti

1. Peel pears. Cut lengthwise into quarters. Cut off cores and stems; discard. Place pears in large skillet.

2. Whisk juice, honey and cinnamon in small bowl; pour over pears. Bring to a boil over medium-high heat. Reduce heat to low; simmer pears about 10 minutes or until tender, turning occasionally to coat evenly. Remove pears from skillet to serving plates with slotted spoon; keep warm.

3. Boil liquid 3 to 4 minutes or until syrupy. Drizzle glaze over pears. Sprinkle with crushed biscotti.   *Makes 4 servings*

Frozen Chocolate Soufflés

3 cups cold milk
1 package (8-serving size) or 2 packages (4-serving size each)
   JELL-O® Chocolate Flavor Instant Pudding & Pie Filling
2 cups thawed COOL WHIP® Whipped Topping
16 OREO® Chocolate Sandwich Cookies, chopped (about 2 cups)
8 maraschino cherries

POUR milk into medium bowl. Add dry pudding mix. Beat with wire whisk 2 minutes. Gently stir in whipped topping.

SPOON 2 tablespoons of the chopped cookies into each of 8 (8- to 9-ounce) paper drinking cups. Cover evenly with half of the pudding mixture. Repeat layers. Cover with foil.

FREEZE 5 hours or until firm. Remove from freezer about 15 minutes before serving. Let stand at room temperature to soften slightly. Peel away paper to unmold soufflés onto plates. Top each with a cherry. Store leftover soufflés in freezer.

Makes 8 servings (1 soufflé each)

Variation: Prepare as directed, using JELL-O® Vanilla Flavor Instant Pudding & Pie Filling and CHIPS AHOY!® Real Chocolate Chip Cookies.

Almond Mini Chip Shortbread

1 cup (2 sticks) butter (no substitutes), softened
½ cup sugar
2½ cups all-purpose flour
1 teaspoon almond extract
1 cup HERSHEY₅'S Mini Chips Semi-Sweet Chocolate

1. Heat oven to 350°F. Grease 13×9×2-inch baking pan.

2. Beat butter and sugar in large bowl until fluffy. Add flour and almond extract; blend well. Stir in small chocolate chips; pat into prepared pan.

3. Bake 30 minutes or until golden brown. Cool 10 minutes; cut into bars. Cool completely in pan on wire rack.

Makes about 3 dozen bars

Baked Caramel Rice Custard

3 cups fat-free milk
½ cup CREAM OF RICE® Hot Cereal, uncooked
1 teaspoon vanilla extract
3 eggs
1 cup sugar, divided
½ teaspoon salt

1. Preheat oven to 325°F. Bring milk just to a boil in medium saucepan over medium heat. Gradually add Cream of Rice, stirring constantly. Cook and stir 1 minute longer. Remove from heat; cover. Let stand 4 minutes. Stir in vanilla.

2. Mix eggs, ⅓ cup sugar and salt until well blended. Add to Cream of Rice mixture and mix well; set aside.

3. Heat remaining ⅔ cup sugar in medium saucepan over medium heat until melted and golden brown, stirring occasionally. Immediately pour into 1½-quart baking dish, tilting dish to evenly coat bottom and sides of dish. Pour cereal mixture into prepared dish. Place in 13×9-inch baking pan; carefully add 2 cups hot water to baking pan.

4. Bake 60 to 70 minutes or until knife inserted in center comes out clean. Cool on wire rack. Unmold onto serving plate. Serve warm or chilled.
Makes 8 servings

Tip: To unmold the custard neatly, run a small knife around the edge of the custard. Place a serving plate over the mold and turn the mold over carefully onto the plate. Let stand at least 30 seconds or until the custard releases onto the plate.

Prep Time: 15 minutes • **Start to Finish Time:** 1 hour 15 minutes

6 Ingredient
cookbook

CONTENTS

EXPRESS-LANE APPETIZERS

Micro Mini Stuffed Potatoes

1 pound small new red potatoes
¼ cup sour cream
2 tablespoons butter, softened
½ teaspoon minced garlic
¼ cup milk
½ cup (2 ounces) shredded sharp Cheddar cheese
½ teaspoon salt
¼ teaspoon black pepper
¼ cup finely chopped green onions

Microwave Directions

1. Pierce potatoes with fork in several places. Microwave potatoes on HIGH 5 to 6 minutes or until tender. Let stand 5 minutes; cut in half lengthwise. Scoop out pulp from potatoes; set potato shells aside.

2. Beat potato pulp in medium bowl with electric mixer at low speed 30 seconds. Add sour cream, butter and garlic; beat until well blended. Gradually add milk, beating until smooth. Add Cheddar, salt and pepper; beat until blended.

3. Fill each potato shell with equal amounts of potato mixture. Microwave on HIGH 1 to 2 minutes or until cheese melts. Sprinkle with green onions. *Makes 4 servings*

Mini Marinated Beef Skewers

1 boneless beef top sirloin (about 1 pound)
2 tablespoons dry sherry
2 tablespoons soy sauce
1 tablespoon dark sesame oil
2 cloves garlic, minced
18 cherry tomatoes

1. Cut beef crosswise into ⅛-inch slices. Place in large resealable food storage bag. Combine sherry, soy sauce, sesame oil and garlic in small bowl; pour over beef. Seal bag; turn to coat. Marinate in refrigerator at least 30 minutes or up to 2 hours. Soak 18 (6-inch) wooden skewers in water 20 minutes.

2. Preheat broiler. Drain beef; discard marinade. Weave beef accordion-style onto skewers. Place on rack of broiler pan.

3. Broil 4 to 5 inches from heat 2 minutes. Turn skewers over; broil 2 minutes or until beef is barely pink in center. Place 1 cherry tomato on each skewer. Serve warm or at room temperature.

Makes 18 appetizers

Deviled Eggs

1 dozen eggs
½ cup plain lowfat STONYFIELD FARM® Yogurt
1 tablespoon Dijon mustard
1 teaspoon lemon juice
1 teaspoon paprika
Fresh chopped chives for garnish

Place eggs in large saucepan and cover with cold water. Bring water to a boil and immediately remove from heat. Cover and let eggs stand in hot water for 10 to 12 minutes. Remove from hot water, cool and peel. Slice eggs in half lengthwise and remove yolks. Place yolks in medium bowl. Mash together with yogurt, mustard and lemon juice. Fill hollowed egg whites generously with egg yolk mixture. Sprinkle with paprika and chives. Refrigerate until ready to serve.

Makes 24 servings

Olive Tapenade

1 can (16 ounces) medium pitted black olives
½ cup pimiento-stuffed green olives
1 tablespoon roasted garlic*
½ teaspoon dry mustard
½ cup (2 ounces) crumbled feta cheese
1 tablespoon olive oil
Toast slices

To roast garlic, preheat oven to 400°F. Remove outer layers of papery skin; cut ¼ inch off top of garlic head. Place cut side up on piece of heavy-duty foil. Drizzle with 2 teaspoons olive oil; wrap tightly in foil. Bake 25 to 30 minutes or until cloves feel soft when pressed. Cool slightly before squeezing out garlic pulp.

1. Process olives, roasted garlic and mustard in food processor or blender until finely chopped.

2. Combine olive mixture, feta and oil in medium bowl; stir until well blended. Serve with toast slices.

Makes 1¾ cups tapenade

Tip: For the best flavor, prepare this tapenade several hours or one day ahead to allow the flavors to blend.

Chili Pepper Baked Tortilla Chips

¼ cup PROMISE® Buttery Spread, melted
½ teaspoon ground chili powder
½ teaspoon LAWRY'S® Garlic Powder with Parsley
½ teaspoon ground cumin
¼ teaspoon ground cayenne pepper
6 (10-inch) burrito-size low-fat flour tortillas

1. Preheat oven to 425°F.

2. In small bowl, blend all ingredients except tortillas. Brush mixture on one side of each tortilla, then cut into 8 wedges. On baking sheet, arrange wedges in a single layer. Bake 8 minutes or until golden and crisp. Serve warm or remove to wire rack and cool. Store in airtight container.

Makes 48 chips

Prep Time: 10 minutes • **Bake Time:** 8 minutes

Mini Reuben Skewers with Dipping Sauce

⅓ cup **HELLMANN'S® or BEST FOODS® Real Mayonnaise**
⅓ cup **WISH-BONE® Thousand Island Dressing**
1 **can (8 ounces) sauerkraut, drained and coarsely chopped**
4 **thin slices rye bread, crust removed**
8 **ounces sliced Swiss cheese**
8 **ounces sliced cooked corned beef or pastrami**

Combine HELLMANN'S® or BEST FOODS® Real Mayonnaise, WISH-BONE® Thousand Island Dressing and sauerkraut in medium bowl; set aside.

Top 2 bread slices evenly with cheese, corned beef, then remaining bread. Cut each sandwich into 20 cubes and secure with wooden toothpicks. Serve with dipping sauce.

Makes 40 servings

Prep Time: 10 minutes

Grilled Bruschetta

3 **tablespoons olive oil**
2 **tablespoons red wine vinegar**
2 **cloves garlic, minced**
½ **teaspoon cracked black pepper**
2 **tablespoons chopped fresh parsley or basil leaves**
2 **medium tomatoes, chopped (about 2 cups)**
1 **package (11.25 ounces) PEPPERIDGE FARM® Texas Toast Parmesan or Garlic Texas Toast**

1. Stir the oil, vinegar, garlic, black pepper, parsley and tomatoes in a medium bowl. Let stand for 15 minutes.

2. Lightly oil the grill rack and heat the grill to medium. Grill the toast slices for 2 minutes or until they're browned on both sides and heated through.

3. Divide the tomato mixture among the toast slices. Serve immediately.

Makes 8 servings

Kitchen Tip: Omit the garlic if using Garlic Texas Toast.

Salmon-Wrapped Snow Peas

16 snow peas
1 tablespoon water
1 package (4 ounces) sliced smoked salmon
1 tablespoon minced fresh chives
¼ cup reduced-sodium soy sauce
2 teaspoons rice vinegar
½ teaspoon sugar
Sesame seeds (optional)

1. Place snow peas and water in small microwavable dish; cover loosely with plastic wrap. Microwave on HIGH 1 to 2 minutes or until crisp-tender.

2. Cut salmon into 16 strips, each 2 to 3 inches long and 1 inch wide. Wrap salmon around snow peas; secure with toothpicks, if desired. Arrange on serving platter; sprinkle with chives.

3. Combine soy sauce, vinegar and sugar in small bowl; stir until sugar is dissolved. Sprinkle sesame seeds over sauce. Serve with snow peas for dipping. *Makes 8 servings*

Philly BBQ Ranch Chicken Dip

1 package (8 ounces) PHILADELPHIA® Neufchâtel Cheese,
⅓ Less Fat than Cream Cheese, softened
¼ cup KRAFT® Barbecue Sauce, any flavor
1 package (6 ounces) OSCAR MAYER® Grilled Chicken Breast
Strips, chopped
2 tablespoons KRAFT® Light Ranch Reduced Fat Dressing
¼ cup chopped red bell pepper
¼ cup sliced green onions

SPREAD Neufchâtel cheese onto bottom of microwavable 9-inch pie plate. Spread barbecue sauce over Neufchâtel cheese. Top with chicken.

MICROWAVE on HIGH (100%) 2 minutes or until heated through. Top with remaining ingredients.

SERVE with WHEAT THINS® Snack Crackers and cut up vegetables.
Makes 2¼ cups or 18 servings (2 tablespoons each)

Tuna Quesadilla Stack

4 (10-inch) flour tortillas
¼ cup plus 2 tablespoons pinto or black bean dip
1 can (about 14 ounces) diced tomatoes, drained
1 can (9 ounces) tuna packed in water, drained and flaked
2 cups (8 ounces) shredded Cheddar cheese
½ cup thinly sliced green onions
1½ teaspoons butter, melted

1. Preheat oven to 400°F.

2. Place 1 tortilla on 12-inch pizza pan. Spread with 2 tablespoons bean dip, leaving ½-inch border. Top with one third each of tomatoes, tuna, Cheddar and green onions. Repeat layers twice, beginning with tortilla and ending with green onions. Top with remaining tortilla, pressing gently. Brush with melted butter.

3. Bake 15 minutes or until cheese melts and top is lightly browned. Cool slightly. Cut into 8 wedges. *Makes 4 servings*

Serving Suggestion: Serve with assorted toppings such as guacamole, sour cream and salsa.

Roast Beef Roll-Ups

1 package (8 ounces) cream cheese, softened
1 cup (4 ounces) crumbled blue cheese
1 teaspoon Dijon mustard
½ teaspoon black pepper
1 pound sliced deli roast beef
1 small red onion, thinly sliced
12 butter lettuce leaves (about 1 head)

1. Mix cream cheese, blue cheese, mustard and pepper in small bowl until well blended.

2. Spread each slice of roast beef with 1 tablespoon cheese mixture. Top with 1 to 2 slices onion and 1 leaf lettuce. Roll up roast beef slices starting at short end; secure with toothpicks, if necessary. Arrange rolls on serving platter. Cover and refrigerate until ready to serve. *Makes about 12 servings*

Marinated Artichoke Cheese Toasts

  1 jar (8 ounces) marinated artichoke hearts, drained
  ½ cup (2 ounces) shredded Swiss cheese
  ⅓ cup finely chopped roasted red peppers
  ⅓ cup finely chopped celery
  2 tablespoons mayonnaise
24 melba toast rounds
    Paprika (optional)

1. Preheat broiler. Finely chop artichokes; place in medium bowl. Add cheese, peppers, celery and mayonnaise; mix well.

2. Spoon artichoke mixture evenly onto melba toast rounds; place on large nonstick baking sheet or broiler pan. Broil 6 inches from heat 45 seconds or until cheese mixture is bubbly and heated through. Garnish with paprika. *Makes 12 servings*

Easy Empanadas

1 cup prepared refrigerated barbecued shredded pork
2 tablespoons ORTEGA® Taco Sauce
1 tablespoon ORTEGA® Fire-Roasted Diced Green Chiles
1 can (12 count) refrigerated biscuits
1 egg, well beaten
1 cup ORTEGA® Black Bean & Corn Salsa

Preheat oven to 375°F. Mix pork, taco sauce and chiles in small bowl.

Separate biscuits into 12 pieces. Flatten each biscuit into 6-inch round using rolling pin. Divide filling evenly among biscuits, spreading over half of each round to within ¼ inch of edge. Fold dough over filling; press edges with fork to seal well. Place on ungreased cookie sheet. Brush tops with beaten egg.

Bake 12 to 15 minutes or until edges are golden brown. Immediately remove from cookie sheet. Serve warm with salsa for dipping. *Makes 12 empanadas*

Prep Time: 10 minutes • **Start to Finish Time:** 25 minutes

Creamy Mushroom Cups

2 tablespoons butter
4 ounces mushrooms, coarsely chopped
¼ teaspoon salt
2 cloves garlic, minced
2 tablespoons dry sherry
¼ cup whipping cream
15 frozen mini phyllo shells, thawed and warmed
¼ cup chopped fresh parsley

1. Melt butter in large nonstick skillet over medium heat. Add mushrooms and salt; cook and stir 3 minutes or until tender. Add garlic; cook and stir 15 seconds.

2. Add sherry; stir to blend. Stir in cream; cook and stir 2 minutes or until thickened.

3. Divide mushroom mixture evenly among phyllo shells. Sprinkle with parsley; serve immediately.   *Makes 5 servings*

Salmon Bites

¼ cup lowfat mayonnaise
2 teaspoons fresh lemon juice
1 can (about 6 ounces) white or pink salmon, drained and flaked
1 medium tomato, cut in half and thinly sliced
4 slices PEPPERIDGE FARM® Very Thin Wheat or White Bread, toasted
¼ cup very thinly sliced red onion

1. Stir the mayonnaise and lemon juice in a medium bowl. Stir in the salmon.

2. Divide the tomato slices and salmon mixture among the toast slices and top with the red onion.

3. Cut the sandwiches diagonally into quarters. Serve immediately.   *Makes 16 appetizers*

Prep Time: 15 minutes

Velveeta® Double-Decker Nachos

6 ounces tortilla chips (about 7 cups)
1 can (15 ounces) chili with beans
½ pound (8 ounces) VELVEETA® Pasteurized Prepared Cheese
    Product, cut into ½-inch cubes
1 medium tomato, finely chopped
¼ cup sliced green onions
⅓ cup BREAKSTONE'S® or KNUDSEN® Sour Cream

ARRANGE half of the chips on large microwavable platter; top with layers of half each of the chili and VELVEETA®. Repeat layers.

MICROWAVE on HIGH 3 to 5 minutes or until VELVEETA® is melted.

TOP with remaining ingredients.   *Makes 6 servings*

Substitute: Prepare as directed, using VELVEETA® Mild Mexican Pasteurized Prepared Cheese Product with Jalapeño Peppers.

Prep Time: 10 minutes • **Total Time:** 15 minutes

Refried Bean and Cheese Quesadillas

1 (16-ounce) can refried beans
1 tablespoon Original TABASCO® brand Pepper Sauce
8 (8-inch) flour tortillas
1 large red bell pepper, finely chopped
¼ cup chopped fresh cilantro or parsley
2 cups (8 ounces) shredded Monterey Jack or Cheddar cheese

Preheat oven to 450°F. Combine refried beans and TABASCO® Sauce in medium bowl; mix well. Spread 3 tablespoons mixture on each tortilla to within ½ inch of edge; sprinkle with red bell pepper, cilantro and cheese. Place tortillas on 2 large cookie sheets.

Bake 5 minutes or until cheese is melted and edges of tortillas are golden. To serve, cut tortillas into wedges.   *Makes 8 servings*

EFFORTLESS ENTRÉES

Zesty Chicken Pot Pie

12 ounces (1½ packages (8 ounces each)) PHILADELPHIA®
    Cream Cheese, cubed
½ cup chicken broth
3 cups chopped cooked chicken
2 packages (10 ounces each) frozen mixed vegetables,
    thawed
1 envelope GOOD SEASONS® Italian Salad Dressing &
    Recipe Mix
1 refrigerated ready-to-use refrigerated pie crust
    (½ of 15-ounce package)

PREHEAT oven to 425°F. Place cream cheese in large saucepan. Add broth; cook on low heat until cream cheese is completely melted, stirring frequently with wire whisk. Stir in chicken, vegetables and salad dressing mix.

SPOON into 9-inch pie plate. Cover with pie crust; seal and flute edge. Cut several slits in crust to allow steam to escape. Place pie plate on baking sheet.

BAKE 20 to 25 minutes or until golden brown.

Makes 8 servings

Serving Suggestion: Serve with a mixed green salad and a glass of fat-free milk.

Make Ahead: Prepare as directed except for baking. Wrap securely; freeze. When ready to bake, unwrap. Place strips of foil around edge to prevent over browning. Bake frozen pie at 425°F for 1 hour and 10 minutes or until heated through.

Substitutes: Prepare as directed, using PHILADELPHIA® Neufchâtel Cheese, ⅓ Less Fat than Cream Cheese, OR GOOD SEASONS® Zesty Italian Dressing OR substituting turkey for the chicken.

Prep Time: 20 minutes • **Bake Time:** 25 minutes

Hearty Pork Stew

2 pounds sweet potatoes, peeled and cut into 2-inch pieces (about 2 cups)
2 pounds boneless pork shoulder roast, cut into 1-inch pieces
1 can (14½ ounces) CAMPBELL'S® Chicken Gravy
1 teaspoon dried thyme leaves, crushed
½ teaspoon crushed red pepper
1 can (15 ounces) black-eyed peas, rinsed and drained

1. Put the potatoes in a 4- to 6-quart slow cooker. Top with the pork.

2. Stir the gravy, thyme, red pepper and peas in a small bowl. Pour over the pork and potatoes.

3. Cover and cook on LOW for 7 to 8 hours* or until the meat is fork-tender. *Makes 8 servings*

*Or on HIGH for 4 to 5 hours.

Prep Time: 25 minutes • **Cook Time:** 7 to 8 hours

Hoisin-Orange Chicken Wraps

¼ cup hoisin sauce
½ teaspoon grated orange peel
¼ cup orange juice
8 whole Boston lettuce leaves
2 cups shredded coleslaw mix
2 cups diced cooked chicken (about 8 ounces)
¼ cup sliced green onions
    Black pepper

1. Combine hoisin sauce, orange peel and juice in small bowl.

2. Arrange lettuce leaves on large serving platter. Place ¼ cup coleslaw mix, ¼ cup chicken and 1 tablespoon hoisin mixture on each leaf. Sprinkle with green onions and pepper. Fold lettuce over filling to create wrap. *Makes 4 servings*

Amazin' Crab Rice Cakes

1 cup chicken broth
1 cup MINUTE® White Rice, uncooked
2 eggs
2 cans (6 ounces each) crabmeat, drained, flaked*
2 tablespoons seafood seasoning
¼ cup (½ stick) butter or margarine
Fresh lemon wedges (optional)

Or substitute 12 ounces canned salmon.

Bring broth to a boil in small saucepan. Stir in rice; cover. Remove from heat; let stand 5 minutes. Fluff with fork.

Beat eggs lightly in medium bowl. Add rice, crabmeat and seasoning; mix well. Refrigerate 5 minutes. Shape into 8 patties.

Melt butter in large skillet over medium heat. Add patties; cook 5 minutes on each side or until golden brown and heated through. Serve with lemon, if desired.   *Makes 4 servings*

Tip: To serve as appetizers, make the patties in bite-size portions.

Penne Pasta with Chunky Tomato Sauce and Spinach

1 package (8 ounces) multigrain penne pasta
2 cups spicy marinara sauce
1 large ripe tomato, chopped (about 1½ cups)
4 cups packed baby spinach or torn spinach leaves
¼ cup grated Parmesan cheese
¼ cup chopped fresh basil

1. Cook pasta according to package directions.

2. Meanwhile, heat marinara sauce and tomato in medium saucepan over medium heat 3 to 4 minutes or until hot and bubbly, stirring occasionally. Remove from heat; stir in spinach.

3. Drain pasta; return to same saucepan. Add sauce; toss to combine. Top with Parmesan and basil.   *Makes 4 servings*

Chicago Deep Dish Pizza

1 package (10 ounces) refrigerated pizza dough
¾ cup pizza sauce
1 package (approximately 1 pound) JOHNSONVILLE® Italian
    Sausage Links, casings removed or 1 package
    JOHNSONVILLE® Italian Ground Sausage, browned
    and drained*
1 package (10 ounces) frozen chopped spinach, thawed
    and well drained
⅓ cup shredded Parmesan cheese
1½ cups (6 ounces) shredded mozzarella cheese

Also great with Johnsonville® Italian Sausage, cooked and coin sliced.

Place dough in greased 9-inch round baking pan, securing dough
to top edge of pan. Pierce bottom with fork and bake at 425°F
for 8 to 10 minutes or until lightly browned. Layer crust with half
of the pizza sauce, cooked sausage, spinach, Parmesan cheese
and mozzarella cheese. Repeat layers. Bake at 425°F for 15 to
20 minutes or until cheese is melted and lightly browned. Let
stand 5 minutes before cutting into wedges.   *Makes 6 servings*

Crispy Lemon Fish Fillets

1⅓ cups *French's®* French Fried Onions
½ teaspoon grated lemon zest
½ teaspoon garlic powder
¼ cup flour
4 (½-inch thick) flounder fillets
1 egg, beaten

1. Place French Fried Onions, lemon zest and garlic powder
in plastic bag. Crush onions with hands or rolling pin; shake to
combine.

2. Place flour in another plastic bag. Add fillets; shake to coat.
Dip fillets into egg, then into onion crumbs. Place on baking sheet.

3. Bake at 400°F for 10 minutes or until fish flakes easily with fork.
Makes 4 servings

Tortilla Beef Casserole

1 package (about 17 ounces) refrigerated fully cooked beef
  pot roast in gravy*
6 (6-inch) corn tortillas, cut into 1-inch pieces
1 jar (16 ounces) salsa
1½ cups corn
1 cup canned black or pinto beans, rinsed and drained
1 cup (4 ounces) shredded Mexican cheese blend

*Fully cooked beef pot roast can be found in the refrigerated prepared
meats section of the supermarket.*

1. Preheat oven to 350°F. Lightly spray 11×7-inch baking dish or
2-quart casserole with nonstick cooking spray.

2. Drain and discard gravy from pot roast. Cut or shred beef into
bite-size pieces.

3. Combine beef, tortillas, salsa, corn and beans in large bowl;
mix well. Transfer to prepared dish. Bake 20 minutes or until
heated through. Sprinkle with cheese; bake 5 minutes or
until cheese is melted. *Makes 4 servings*

Weeknight Chili

1 pound ground beef or turkey
1 package (1¼ ounces) chili seasoning mix
1 can (about 15 ounces) red kidney beans, rinsed and drained
1 can (about 14 ounces) diced tomatoes with green chiles
1 can (8 ounces) tomato sauce
1 cup (4 ounces) shredded Cheddar cheese
Sliced green onions (optional)

Slow Cooker Directions

1. Brown beef in large skillet over medium-high heat, stirring
to break up meat. Drain fat. Stir in seasoning mix.

2. Place beef mixture, beans, tomatoes and tomato sauce
in slow cooker. Cover; cook on LOW 4 to 6 hours. Top with
Cheddar and green onions, if desired. *Makes 4 servings*

Bacon & Tomato Presto Pasta

8 slices OSCAR MAYER® Bacon, chopped
½ cup cherry tomatoes
**1 tub (8 ounces) PHILADELPHIA® Chive & Onion Cream Cheese
     Spread**
1 cup milk
½ cup KRAFT® 100% Grated Parmesan Cheese
6 cups hot cooked penne pasta

COOK bacon in skillet 5 minutes or until bacon is crisp, stirring occasionally. Drain skillet, leaving bacon in skillet. Stir in cherry tomatoes.

ADD cream cheese spread, milk and Parmesan cheese; mix well. Cook until hot and bubbly, stirring frequently.

STIR in pasta.   *Makes 8 servings*

Prep Time: 10 minutes • **Cook Time:** 10 minutes

Currant Glazed Ham

1 ready-to-eat ham (5 pounds)
¾ cup red currant jelly
½ cup KARO® Dark Corn Syrup
1 teaspoon vinegar
½ teaspoon ground cloves
1 teaspoon whole cloves

Trim and heat ham as directed on package.

Combine jelly, corn syrup, vinegar and ground cloves in saucepan. Cook over medium-low heat, stirring constantly, until jelly is melted and mixture is smooth.

Remove ham from oven; score diagonally, making cuts about 1 inch deep and about ¾ inch apart, across fat surface of ham.

Stud with whole cloves, placing one in center of each diamond.

Pour part of glaze over ham. Bake at 325°F about 45 minutes, basting frequently with remaining glaze, until ham is well coated and all glaze is used. Serve with pan juices as a sauce.

Makes 1¼ cups glaze

Warm Spinach and Rice Chicken Salad

2 TYSON® Individually Frozen Boneless Skinless Chicken Breasts, frozen
⅓ cup Italian salad dressing, divided
1 box chicken-flavored rice
4 cups chopped fresh spinach
2 plum tomatoes, chopped
¼ cup pitted ripe olives, halved

1. Wash hands. Remove protective ice glaze from frozen chicken by holding under cool running water 1 to 2 minutes. Brush chicken with 2 teaspoons salad dressing. Wash hands.

2. Grill or broil chicken, turning once, 20 to 25 minutes or until internal juices of chicken run clear. (Or insert instant-read meat thermometer into thickest part of chicken. Temperature should read 180°F.)

3. Meanwhile, prepare rice according to package directions. Combine hot cooked rice with remaining salad dressing, spinach, tomatoes and olives; stir until spinach is slightly wilted.

4. Place rice mixture on individual serving plates; top with sliced chicken. Refrigerate leftovers immediately.   *Makes 2 servings*

Sausage Stew

1 pound BOB EVANS® Italian Sausage Roll
2 cans (14½ ounces each) Italian-style diced tomatoes
2 cans (14½ ounces each) beef broth
1 can (16 ounces) red kidney beans, drained and rinsed
1 bag (16 ounces) frozen Italian blend vegetables
1 bag (8 ounces) egg noodles

In a Dutch oven, crumble and cook sausage over medium heat until browned; drain. Add tomatoes, beef broth, beans, frozen vegetables and noodles. Bring to a boil. Stir and reduce heat to low. Cook 7 to 10 minutes or until vegetables and noodles are tender, stirring occasionally.   *Makes 4 to 6 servings*

Cavemen Beef Back Ribs

¼ **cup paprika**
¼ **cup brown sugar**
¼ **cup seasoned salt**
2 **full racks beef back ribs, split in half (6 to 8 pounds)**
1 **cup** *Cattlemen's*® **Authentic Smoke House Barbecue Sauce**
¼ **cup apple, pineapple or orange juice**

1. Combine paprika, sugar and seasoned salt. Rub mixture into ribs. Cover ribs and refrigerate 1 to 3 hours.

2. Prepare grill for indirect cooking over medium-low heat (250°F). Place ribs on rib rack or in foil pan. Cook on covered grill 2½ to 3 hours until very tender.

3. Meanwhile, combine barbecue sauce and juice. Brush mixture on ribs during last 30 minutes of cooking. Serve with additional barbecue sauce. *Makes 6 to 8 servings*

Tip: For very tender ribs, remove the membrane from the underside before cooking. Score the membrane on the bone from the underside of the ribs with a sharp paring knife. Lift up portions of the membrane with the point of a knife. Using a kitchen towel, pull the membrane away from the bone and discard.

Classic Reuben

2 **slices rye bread**
1 **tablespoon WISH-BONE® Ranch Dressing**
¼ **cup sauerkraut, drained**
1 **ounce thinly sliced Swiss cheese**
3 **ounces thinly sliced corned beef**
1 **tablespoon HELLMANN'S® or BEST FOODS® Real Mayonnaise**

Spread bread evenly with WISH-BONE® Ranch Dressing, then top with remaining ingredients except Mayonnaise. Evenly spread Mayonnaise on outside of sandwich.

Cook sandwich in 8-inch nonstick skillet, turning once and pressing down, 7 minutes or until golden brown and cheese is melted.
Makes 1 serving

Quick and Easy Sautéed Chicken

4 boneless skinless chicken breasts
1 teaspoon paprika (preferably smoked)
1 teaspoon dried thyme
1 teaspoon dried parsley flakes
½ teaspoon garlic salt
⅛ teaspoon ground red pepper
1 tablespoon olive oil

1. Place chicken breasts between sheets of waxed paper or plastic wrap; pound to even ½-inch thickness. Combine paprika, thyme, parsley, garlic salt and red pepper in small bowl; rub over both sides of chicken.

2. Heat oil in large nonstick skillet over medium heat. Add chicken; cook 4 to 5 minutes per side or until chicken is no longer pink in center. Pour any juices from skillet over chicken.

Makes 4 servings

Huevos Rancheros Casserole

6 corn tortillas
1 cup refried black beans
1 cup salsa
10 eggs
¾ cup milk
1 cup (4 ounces) shredded Mexican cheese blend

1. Preheat oven to 400°F. Spray 13×9-inch baking dish with nonstick cooking spray. Line prepared dish with tortillas, overlapping as necessary to fit. Spread beans evenly over tortillas; spread salsa evenly over beans.

2. Whisk eggs and milk in large bowl until well blended. Pour over salsa; top with cheese. Cover dish with foil.

3. Bake 30 minutes. Remove foil; bake 5 minutes more or until center is set and edges are lightly browned and pulling away from sides of dish. *Makes 6 to 8 servings*

Serving Suggestion: Serve with additional salsa, sour cream, chopped fresh cilantro and sliced avocado.

Chipotle Roast Beef Sandwich with Pepper Jack

1 tablespoon HELLMANN'S® or BEST FOODS® Light Mayonnaise
¼ teaspoon ground chipotle chile pepper
1 seeded Kaiser roll, split
3 ounces thinly sliced deli roast beef
1 ounce sliced pepper jack cheese
¼ cup watercress or lettuce

Combine HELLMANN'S® or BEST FOODS® Light Mayonnaise with chile pepper in small bowl; spread on bottom half of roll. Top with roast beef, cheese and watercress, then top half of roll.

Makes 1 serving

Roast Chicken with Peppers

1 chicken (3 to 3½ pounds), cut into pieces
3 tablespoons olive oil, divided
2 tablespoons lemon juice
1 tablespoon plus 1½ teaspoons chopped fresh rosemary
  leaves *or* 1½ teaspoons dried rosemary
1¼ teaspoons salt, divided
¾ teaspoon black pepper, divided
3 bell peppers (red, yellow and/or green), cut into ½-inch strips
1 medium onion, cut into thin wedges

1. Preheat oven to 375°F. Place chicken in shallow roasting pan.

2. Combine 2 tablespoons oil, lemon juice and rosemary in small bowl; brush over chicken. Sprinkle 1 teaspoon salt and ½ teaspoon black pepper over chicken. Roast 15 minutes.

3. Toss bell peppers and onion with remaining 1 tablespoon oil, ¼ teaspoon salt and ¼ teaspoon black pepper in medium bowl. Spoon vegetables around chicken; roast about 40 minutes or until vegetables are tender and chicken is cooked through (165°F).

Makes 6 servings

SPEEDY SIDE DISHES

Spinach Salad with Italian Marinated Mushrooms & Gorgonzola

½ cup WISH-BONE® Italian or Light Italian Dressing, divided
1 package (10 ounces) cremini or white mushrooms, washed and stems trimmed
1 small red onion, sliced into ½-inch rounds
1 package (10 ounces) baby spinach or (4 ounces) baby arugula
1 package (4 ounces) gorgonzola cheese crumbles*
4 slices bacon, crisp-cooked and crumbled
Freshly ground black pepper (optional)

*Also terrific with blue cheese crumbles.

Pour ¼ cup WISH-BONE® Italian Dressing over mushrooms and onion in medium nonaluminum baking dish or resealable plastic bag. Cover or close bag, and marinate in refrigerator, turning occasionally, at least 30 minutes.

Remove vegetables from marinade, reserving marinade. Grill or broil vegetables, brushing with reserved marinade, 15 minutes or until tender. Quarter mushrooms and chop onion; let stand covered in medium bowl, then toss with remaining ¼ cup Dressing.

Toss spinach, mushroom mixture with juices, cheese and bacon in large serving bowl or platter. Sprinkle with black pepper.

Makes 6 servings

Prep Time: 15 minutes • **Marinate Time:** 30 minutes •
Cook Time: 15 minutes

Easy Mock Twice-Baked Potatoes

2 strips bacon
1 package SIMPLY POTATOES® Country Style Mashed Potatoes
½ cup chive and onion soft cream cheese
¾ teaspoon salt
⅓ cup CRYSTAL FARMS® Shredded Cheddar cheese
Paprika
Chopped fresh chives

1. Heat oven to 350°F. In 10-inch skillet, cook bacon on medium-high heat until crisp. Drain grease; crumble bacon. In medium bowl, combine **Simply Potatoes®**, cream cheese, bacon and salt; stir to mix well. Spoon about ⅔ cup **Simply Potatoes®** mixture into 6 (1-cup) glass custard cups or ramekins. Top each with 1 tablespoon cheese. Sprinkle tops with dash of paprika.

2. Bake 15 to 20 minutes or until heated through. Garnish with chopped fresh chives. *Makes 6 servings*

Prep Time: 10 minutes • **Bake Time:** 15 minutes

Hot and Spicy Spinach

1 tablespoon olive oil
1 red bell pepper, cut into 1-inch pieces
1 clove garlic, minced
1 pound fresh spinach, stemmed and chopped
1 tablespoon yellow mustard
1 teaspoon lemon juice
½ teaspoon salt
¼ teaspoon red pepper flakes

1. Heat oil in large skillet over medium heat. Add bell pepper and garlic; cook and stir 3 minutes.

2. Add spinach; cook and stir 3 minutes or just until spinach begins to wilt.

3. Stir in mustard, lemon juice, salt and red pepper flakes. Serve immediately. *Makes 4 servings*

Summer Mixed Grill Vegetable Kabobs

6 medium mushroom caps
1 medium onion, cut into chunks
1 medium green and/or yellow bell pepper, cut into chunks
1 cup cherry or grape tomatoes
½ cup WISH-BONE® Italian Dressing*
1 teaspoon finely chopped fresh dill

Also terrific with WISH-BONE® Light Italian Dressing.

Combine all ingredients in large shallow baking dish. Cover and marinate in refrigerator, turning occasionally, 4 hours or overnight.

Remove vegetables, reserving marinade. Alternately thread vegetables on skewers.* Grill kabobs, turning and basting frequently with reserved marinade, until done.

Makes 6 servings

If using wooden skewers, soak at least 30 minutes prior to use to avoid burning.

Prep Time: 20 minutes • **Marinate Time:** 4 hours • **Cook Time:** 15 minutes

Dijon Rice Florentine

1 can (14½ ounces) chicken broth
1 clove garlic, minced
1 cup MINUTE® White Rice, uncooked
1 package (10 ounces) frozen chopped spinach, thawed, well drained
2 tablespoons Dijon mustard
2 tablespoons Parmesan cheese, grated

Bring broth and garlic to a boil in medium saucepan over high heat. Add rice; stir. Reduce heat to low; cover. Cook 10 minutes.

Add spinach and mustard; stir. Cook, uncovered, an additional 8 to 10 minutes or until liquid is absorbed and rice is tender. Stir in cheese.

Makes 4 servings

Bacon and Cheese Brunch Potatoes

3 medium russet potatoes (about 2 pounds), peeled and
    cut into 1-inch pieces
1 cup chopped onion
½ teaspoon seasoned salt
4 slices crisp-cooked bacon, crumbled
1 cup (4 ounces) shredded sharp Cheddar cheese
1 tablespoon chicken broth or water

Slow Cooker Directions

1. Spray slow cooker with nonstick cooking spray. Place half of potatoes in slow cooker. Sprinkle half of onion and seasoned salt over potatoes; top with half of bacon and Cheddar. Repeat layers, ending with Cheddar. Sprinkle with broth.

2. Cover; cook on LOW 6 hours or on HIGH 3½ hours or until potatoes and onion are tender. Stir gently to mix. Serve hot.

Makes 6 servings

Bubbling Wisconsin Cheese Bread

½ cup (2 ounces) shredded Wisconsin Mozzarella cheese
⅓ cup mayonnaise or salad dressing
⅛ teaspoon garlic powder
⅛ teaspoon onion powder
1 loaf (16 ounces) French bread, halved lengthwise
⅓ cup (1 ounce) grated Wisconsin Parmesan cheese

Preheat oven to 350°F. Combine mozzarella cheese, mayonnaise, garlic powder and onion powder in mixing bowl; mix well (mixture will be very thick). Spread half the mixture over each bread half. Sprinkle half the Parmesan cheese over each half. Bake 20 to 25 minutes or until bubbly and lightly browned.* Cut each half into 8 slices.

Makes 16 servings

To broil, position on rack 4 inches from heat for 3 to 5 minutes.

*Favorite recipe from **Wisconsin Milk Marketing Board***

Glazed Parsnips and Carrots

1 pound parsnips (2 large or 3 medium)
1 package (8 ounces) baby carrots
1 tablespoon canola oil
  Salt and black pepper
¼ cup orange juice
2½ tablespoons butter
1 tablespoon honey
⅛ teaspoon ground ginger

1. Preheat oven to 425°F. Peel parsnips; cut into wedges to match size of baby carrots.

2. Spread vegetables in shallow roasting pan. Drizzle with oil and season with salt and pepper; toss to coat. Roast 30 to 35 minutes or until fork-tender.

3. Combine orange juice, butter, honey and ginger in large skillet. Add roasted vegetables; cook and stir over high heat 1 to 2 minutes or until sauce thickens and coats vegetables.

Makes 6 servings

Corn and Black-Eyed Pea Salad

1 bag (16 ounces) frozen whole kernel corn, thawed
  (about 3 cups)
1 can (about 15 ounces) black-eyed peas, rinsed and drained
1 large green pepper, chopped (about 1 cup)
1 medium onion, chopped (about ½ cup)
½ cup chopped fresh cilantro leaves
1 jar (16 ounces) PACE® Chunky Salsa

1. Place the corn, peas, green pepper, onion and cilantro in a medium bowl. Add the salsa and stir to coat.

2. Cover and refrigerate for 4 hours. Stir before serving.

Makes 8 servings

Kitchen Tip: To make ahead, prepare salad as directed. Cover and refrigerate overnight. Stir before serving.

Mama's Best Baked Beans

1 bag (1 pound) dried Great Northern beans
1 package (1 pound) bacon
5 hot dogs, cut into ½-inch pieces
1 cup chopped onion
1 bottle (24 ounces) ketchup
2 cups dark brown sugar

Slow Cooker Directions

1. Soak and cook beans according to package directions. Drain and refrigerate until ready to use.

2. Cook bacon in skillet over medium-high heat until crisp. Drain on paper towels. Crumble bacon and set aside. Discard all but 3 tablespoons bacon fat from skillet. Add hot dogs and onion; cook and stir over medium heat until onion is tender.

3. Combine cooked beans, bacon, hot dog mixture, ketchup and brown sugar in slow cooker. Cover; cook on LOW 2 to 4 hours.

Makes 8 to 10 servings

Scalloped Potatoes with Gorgonzola

1½ cups whipping cream
1 can (14½ ounces) chicken broth
4 teaspoons minced garlic
1½ teaspoons sage
1 cup BELGIOIOSO® Gorgonzola
2¼ pounds russet potatoes, peeled, halved, thinly sliced

Preheat oven to 375°F. Simmer whipping cream, chicken broth, garlic and sage in heavy medium saucepan 5 minutes until slightly thickened. Add BELGIOIOSO® Gorgonzola and stir until melted. Remove from heat.

Season potatoes with salt and pepper. Arrange half of potatoes in 13×9×2-inch glass baking dish. Pour half of cream mixture over potatoes. Repeat layering with remaining potatoes and cream mixture. Bake until potatoes are tender, about 1¼ hours. Let stand 15 minutes before serving.

Makes 8 servings

Apple Pecan Stuffing

½ **cup (1 stick) butter**
1 **large onion, chopped**
1 **large Granny Smith apple, peeled and diced**
2½ **cups chicken broth**
1 **package (16 ounces) corn bread stuffing mix**
½ **cup chopped pecans, toasted**

1. Preheat oven to 325°F. Spray 2- to 3-quart casserole with nonstick cooking spray.

2. Melt butter in large saucepan. Add onion; cook 5 minutes, stirring occasionally. Add apple; cook 1 minute. Add broth; bring to a boil. Remove from heat; stir in stuffing mix and pecans.

3. Place stuffing in prepared casserole. Cover and bake 45 minutes or until hot.   *Makes 10 to 12 servings*

Note: Stuffing may be prepared up to 1 day ahead. Store covered in the refrigerator. Let stand at room temperature 30 minutes before baking.

Oven-Roasted Asparagus with Parmesan Gremolata

2 **teaspoons finely chopped fresh parsley**
2 **teaspoons grated Parmesan cheese**
¼ **teaspoon grated lemon peel**
¾ **pound asparagus, trimmed**
2 **large shallots, cut into thin wedges or** ⅓ **cup thinly sliced onion**
1 **tablespoon PROMISE® Buttery Spread, melted**

Preheat oven to 425°F. Combine parsley, cheese and lemon peel in small bowl; set aside.

Toss asparagus, shallots and PROMISE® Buttery Spread in 13×9-inch roasting pan. Roast 15 minutes or until tender.

Arrange asparagus mixture on serving platter, then top with cheese mixture. Season, if desired, with freshly ground black pepper.
Makes 2 servings

Asian Rice & Squash Noodles with Peanut Sauce

1 medium spaghetti squash
2 boxes UNCLE BEN'S® COUNTRY INN® Oriental Fried Rice
4 tablespoons peanut butter
2 tablespoons soy sauce
1 tablespoon grated gingerroot
6 green onions, sliced

PREP: Wash hands. Carefully cut squash in half lengthwise. Remove seeds and place flesh-side down in microwavable baking dish. Add ½ cup water; cover with plastic wrap.

COOK: Microwave squash at HIGH 9 to 10 minutes or until skin is firm but soft. Remove from dish and allow to cool until safe to handle. Spoon out flesh into bowl (it will come out in strands like spaghetti). Meanwhile, prepare rice according to package directions. In large nonstick skillet, combine peanut butter, soy sauce and gingerroot. Heat slightly; add squash and rice. Mix thoroughly.

SERVE: Garnish rice and squash mixture with green onions.

CHILL: Refrigerate leftovers immediately.   *Makes 6 servings*

Tip: Squash can also be baked in 350°F oven 45 to 50 minutes (omit plastic wrap).

Prep Time: 5 minutes • **Cook Time:** 25 minutes

Choose a spaghetti squash that is heavy for
its size, with a hard, smooth pale yellow shell
and no bruises or soft spots. Squash
can be stored at room temperature
for about one month.

DELICIOUS DESSERTS

Mini Oreo® Surprise Cupcakes

1 package (2-layer size) chocolate cake mix
1 package (8 ounces) PHILADELPHIA® Cream Cheese, softened
1 egg
2 tablespoons sugar
48 Mini OREO® Bite Size Chocolate Sandwich Cookies
1½ cups thawed COOL WHIP® Whipped Topping

PREHEAT oven to 350°F. Prepare cake batter as directed on package; set aside. Beat cream cheese, egg and sugar until well blended.

SPOON cake batter into 24 paper- or foil-lined 2½-inch muffin cups, filling each cup about half full. Top each with about 1½ teaspoons of the cream cheese mixture and 1 cookie. Cover evenly with remaining cake batter.

BAKE 19 to 22 minutes or until wooden toothpick inserted in centers comes out clean. Cool 5 minutes; remove from pans to wire racks. Cool completely. (There may be an indentation in top of each cupcake after baking.) Top cupcakes with whipped topping and remaining cookies just before serving. Store in tightly covered container in refrigerator up to 3 days.

Makes 24 servings (1 cupcake each)

Make it Easy: For easy portioning of cream cheese mixture into cake batter, spoon cream cheese mixture into large resealable plastic bag. Seal bag securely. Snip small corner of bag with scissors. Squeeze about 1½ teaspoons of the cream cheese mixture over batter in each muffin cup.

Prep Time: 10 minutes • **Bake Time:** 22 minutes

Dark Molten Chocolate Cakes

1 package (6 squares) BAKER'S® Bittersweet Baking Chocolate
10 tablespoons butter
1½ cups powdered sugar
½ cup flour
3 whole eggs
3 egg yolks
Powdered sugar and raspberries (optional)

PREHEAT oven to 425°F. Grease 6 (6-ounce) custard cups or soufflé dishes. Place on baking sheet.

MICROWAVE chocolate and butter in large microwavable bowl on HIGH 2 minutes or until butter is melted. Stir until chocolate is completely melted. Add powdered sugar and flour; mix well. Add whole eggs and egg yolks; stir with wire whisk until well blended. Divide batter evenly among prepared custard cups.

BAKE 14 to 15 minutes or until cakes are firm around the edges but soft in the centers. Let stand 1 minute. Run small knife around cakes to loosen. Immediately invert cakes onto serving plate. Sprinkle lightly with additional powdered sugar and garnish with raspberries, if desired. Cut each cake in half to serve.

Makes 12 servings (1 cake half each)

Nutty Cheesecake Bites

1 package (8 ounces) cream cheese, softened
½ cup SKIPPY® Creamy Peanut Butter or SKIPPY® SUPER CHUNK® Peanut Butter
¼ cup sugar
¼ teaspoon ground cinnamon
¼ teaspoon vanilla extract
Finely chopped peanuts or unsweetened shredded coconut

1. In medium bowl, with electric mixer on medium speed, combine all ingredients except peanuts, scraping down side of bowl as needed. Chill 30 minutes or until firm.

2. Roll into ¾-inch balls, then roll in peanuts. Chill an additional 15 minutes before serving.

Makes 30 bites

Fig and Camembert Ravioli with Honey Balsamic Glaze

1 package (17.3 ounces) PEPPERIDGE FARM® Frozen Puff Pastry
    Sheets (2 sheets)
1 egg
1 tablespoon water
1 package (8 ounces) Camembert or Brie cheese, cut into
    24 small wedges
12 dried figs, cut in half
    Honey Balsamic Glaze (recipe follows)

1. Thaw the pastry sheets at room temperature for 40 minutes or until they're easy to handle. Heat the oven to 375°F. Lightly grease or line 2 baking sheets with parchment paper. Beat the egg and water in a small bowl with a fork.

2. Unfold **1** pastry sheet on a lightly floured surface. Roll the pastry sheet into a 16-inch square. Brush the pastry sheet with the egg mixture. Arrange the cheese on the pastry in **4** rows with **6** pieces in **each** row. Top **each** cheese piece with **1** fig half.

3. Unfold the remaining pastry sheet on a lightly floured surface. Roll the pastry sheet into a 16-inch square. Place the pastry sheet over the cheese-covered sheet, pressing firmly between the rows and around the edges to seal. Brush the pastry with the egg mixture. Cut between the 4 rows using a fluted pastry wheel or sharp knife to make **4** strips. Cut **each** strip into **6** squares. Place the ravioli onto the baking sheets. Refrigerate for 15 minutes or until the ravioli are firm.

4. Bake for 20 minutes or until the ravioli are golden. Remove the ravioli from the baking sheets and cool on wire racks for 5 minutes. Serve warm with the Honey Balsamic Glaze.   *Makes 24 pieces*

Honey Balsamic Glaze: Heat ¾ cup balsamic vinegar, ½ cup water and ⅓ cup honey in a 2-quart saucepan over high heat to a boil. Reduce the heat to low. Cook for 12 minutes or until the mixture is reduced by half and has a syrup-like consistency.

Kitchen Tip: Substitute ½ cup prepared fig jam or paste for the dried figs. Place about 1 teaspoon onto each cheese piece as directed above in Step 2.

Chilly Chocolate-Mint Parfaits

2 cups cold fat-free milk
1 package (4-serving size) JELL-O® Chocolate Flavor Fat Free
   Sugar Free Instant Reduced Calorie Pudding & Pie Filling
   Few drops peppermint extract
   Few drops green food coloring
1 cup thawed COOL WHIP® Sugar Free Whipped Topping
2 packs (.81 ounce each) 100 CALORIE PACKS OREO® Thin
   Crisps, coarsely broken

POUR milk into medium bowl. Add dry pudding mix and extract. Beat with wire whisk 2 minutes or until well blended. Refrigerate 10 minutes.

STIR food coloring into whipped topping. Layer half each of the pudding mixture, whipped topping and OREO® Crisp pieces in 4 (10-ounce) parfait glasses. Repeat layers of pudding mixture and whipped topping.

REFRIGERATE at least 30 minutes. Sprinkle with remaining OREO® Crisp pieces just before serving.   *Makes 4 servings (1 parfait each)*

Maple Glazed Apples

2 tablespoons mixed chopped dried fruit
4 tablespoons warm water, divided
2 medium cooking apples, halved and cored
⅓ cup maple syrup, divided
2 tablespoons chopped walnuts
¼ cup apple juice
¼ teaspoon ground cinnamon

1. Preheat oven to 350°F. Combine dried fruit and 1 tablespoon water in small bowl. Arrange apples, cut sides up, in 8-inch square baking dish. Brush cut sides of apples with 2 tablespoons syrup.

2. Stir walnuts into dried fruit. Fill centers of apples with fruit mixture. Combine remaining 3 tablespoons water and apple juice in small bowl; pour into baking dish around apples.

3. Bake, uncovered, 45 to 55 minutes or until apples are tender. Spoon apples into serving dishes; drizzle with remaining syrup and sprinkle with cinnamon.   *Makes 4 servings*

Citrus Coolers

1 package (about 18 ounces) lemon cake mix
1 cup (4 ounces) pecan pieces
½ cup all-purpose flour
½ cup (1 stick) butter, melted
   Grated peel and juice of 1 large orange
½ cup powdered sugar

1. Preheat oven to 375°F. Line cookie sheets with parchment paper.

2. Beat cake mix, pecans, flour, butter, orange peel and juice in large bowl with electric mixer at medium speed until well blended. Drop dough by rounded tablespoonfuls 2 inches apart onto prepared cookie sheets.

3. Bake 13 to 15 minutes or until bottoms are golden brown. Cool on cookie sheets 3 minutes; sprinkle with powdered sugar. Remove to wire racks; cool completely.   *Makes about 4½ dozen cookies*

Ice Cream Choco Tacos

8 ORTEGA® Taco Shells
2 cups milk chocolate chips
1 quart vanilla ice cream
½ cup caramel ice cream topping
½ cup chocolate ice cream topping
1 cup chopped nuts

Preheat oven to 325°F. Line cookie sheet with waxed paper. Heat taco shells as directed on package.

Microwave chocolate chips 1 minute in medium microwave-safe bowl on HIGH (100% power). Stir; microwave 30 seconds longer. Repeat until chips melt completely; stir until smooth.

Hold taco shells on bottom. Using butter knife or pastry brush, coat each shell with chocolate inside and out, except for outside bottom edge. Stand shells upright on waxed paper. Refrigerate 30 minutes or until chocolate sets.

Fill each shell with ½ cup ice cream. Drizzle with caramel topping, chocolate topping and nuts, as desired. Serve immediately.
Makes 8 tacos

French Silk Tart

**1½ cups finely chopped chocolate sandwich cookies
    (about 15 cookies)**
⅓ cup butter, melted
1½ cups whipping cream
1 cup semisweet chocolate chips
1 tablespoon unsweetened Dutch process cocoa powder
2 cups whipped topping
Grated chocolate (optional)

1. Combine cookie crumbs and butter in small bowl; mix well. Press firmly on bottom of 10-inch springform pan. Refrigerate until ready to fill.

2. For filling, microwave cream in medium microwavable bowl on HIGH 1 to 1½ minutes or just until hot and bubbles appear around edge. Add chocolate chips; stir until melted. Add cocoa; mix well. Refrigerate 1 hour or until cold and slightly thickened.

3. Beat chilled chocolate mixture with electric mixer at medium speed just until soft peaks form. *Do not overbeat.*

4. Spread chocolate mixture over crust. Spread whipped topping over chocolate layer. Garnish with grated chocolate.

Makes 12 servings

Natural unsweetened cocoa powder may
be substituted for the Dutch process
cocoa, if desired. Dutch process cocoa
has a stronger flavor and will give
desserts a darker color.

Taffy Apple Bars

1 package (16 ounces) refrigerated sugar cookie dough
1 package (16 ounces) refrigerated peanut butter cookie dough
½ cup all-purpose flour
3½ to 4 cups chopped cored peeled apples (about 2 large)
1 cup chopped peanuts
½ cup caramel ice cream topping

1. Preheat oven to 350°F. Lightly grease 13×9-inch baking pan. Let doughs stand at room temperature 15 minutes.

2. Beat doughs and flour in large bowl with electric mixer at medium speed until well blended. Press dough into bottom of prepared pan. Layer apples evenly over dough; press down lightly. Sprinkle with peanuts.

3. Bake 35 minutes or until edges are browned and center is firm to the touch. Cool completely in pan on wire rack. Drizzle with caramel topping. Cut into bars.   *Makes about 2 dozen bars*

Chewy Peanut Butter Blossoms

48 HERSHEY'S KISSES® BRAND Milk Chocolates
1 can (14 ounces) sweetened condensed milk
      (not evaporated milk)
¾ cup REESE'S® Creamy Peanut Butter
2 cups all-purpose biscuit baking mix
1 teaspoon vanilla extract
      About ¼ cup sugar

1. Heat oven to 375°F. Remove wrappers from chocolates.

2. Beat sweetened condensed milk and peanut butter in large bowl until smooth. Add baking mix and vanilla; blend well. Shape into 1-inch balls; roll in sugar. Place 2 inches apart on ungreased cookie sheets.

3. Bake 6 to 8 minutes or until very lightly browned (do not overbake). Remove from oven; immediately press chocolate piece into center of each ball. Remove from cookie sheet to wire rack. Cool completely. Store in tightly covered container.
                                    Makes about 48 cookies

Glazed Plum Pastry

3 tablespoons sugar, divided
2 tablespoons all-purpose flour
1 package (17¼ ounces) frozen puff pastry sheets, thawed
8 plums (about 2 pounds)
¼ teaspoon ground cinnamon
⅓ cup apricot preserves

1. Preheat oven to 400°F. Line 18×12-inch baking sheet with parchment paper. Combine 2 tablespoons sugar and flour in small bowl.

2. Unfold pastry sheets on prepared baking sheet. Place pastry sheets side by side so fold lines are parallel to length of baking sheet and sheets overlap ½ inch in center. Press center seam firmly to seal. Trim ends from length of pastry to 17 inches. (Discard trimmings.) Prick entire surface of pastry with fork.

3. Sprinkle sugar-flour mixture evenly over pastry to within ½ inch of edges. Bake 12 to 15 minutes or until pastry is slightly puffed and golden.

4. Slice plums in half (from stem end to blossom tip); remove pits. Cut plum halves crosswise into ⅛-inch-thick slices. Arrange plum slices slightly overlapping in 5 rows down length of pastry. Combine remaining 1 tablespoon sugar and cinnamon in small bowl; sprinkle evenly over plums.

5. Bake 15 minutes or until plums are tender and pastry is lightly browned. Remove to wire rack.

6. Place preserves in small microwavable bowl; microwave on HIGH 30 to 40 seconds or until melted. Brush preserves over plums. Cool 10 to 15 minutes before serving.   *Makes about 12 servings*

Chocolate Truffle Mousse Bars

- 1 package (6 squares) BAKER'S SELECT® Semi-Sweet Chocolate, divided
- ¼ cup whipping cream
- 2 eggs
- ¼ cup sugar
- 2 tablespoons flour
- 1½ cups thawed COOL WHIP® Whipped Topping

HEAT oven to 325°F. Line 8-inch square pan with greased foil. Microwave 3 chocolate squares and cream in microwavable bowl on HIGH 1 minute. Whisk until chocolate is completely melted; cool. Add eggs, sugar and flour; mix well. Pour into pan.

BAKE 20 minutes or until toothpick inserted in center comes out clean. Cool. Meanwhile, melt 2 chocolate squares as directed on package; cool.

STIR whipped topping into melted chocolate; spread onto dessert. Refrigerate 1 hour. Use ends of foil to lift dessert from pan. Cut into bars. Melt remaining chocolate square; drizzle over bars.

Makes 18 servings

Creamy Baked Custard

- 2½ cups half-and-half
- 2 eggs, lightly beaten
- ¼ cup sugar
- 2 teaspoons vanilla
  - Dash ground nutmeg
- 3 cups boiling water
- 2 tablespoons maple syrup

1. Preheat oven to 325°F. Lightly spray 6 custard cups with nonstick cooking spray. Whisk half-and-half, eggs, sugar, vanilla and nutmeg in large bowl until well blended. Pour into prepared custard cups. Pour boiling water into 13×9-inch baking pan; place cups in pan.

2. Bake 1 hour and 15 minutes. (Centers will not be completely set.) Remove cups from pan; cool completely on wire rack. Cover with plastic wrap; refrigerate overnight. Drizzle with maple syrup before serving.

Makes 6 servings

Lemon Cheesecake Tartlets

**1 package (17.3 ounces) PEPPERIDGE FARM® Frozen Puff Pastry
  Sheets (2 sheets)**
1 egg, beaten
½ of an 8-ounce package cream cheese, softened
½ cup lemon curd
½ cup thawed frozen whipped topping
  Fresh raspberries

1. Thaw the pastry sheets at room temperature for 40 minutes or until they're easy to handle. Heat the oven to 375°F. Lightly grease 24 (2½-inch) muffin pan cups.

2. Unfold **1** pastry sheet onto a lightly floured surface. Roll the sheet into a 12×9-inch rectangle. Cut pastry into 12 (3-inch) squares. Press squares into prepared muffin pan cups. Brush top edges of pastry with egg. Repeat with remaining pastry sheet.

3. Bake for 10 minutes or until golden brown. Cool in pans on wire racks for 5 minutes. Remove pastry cups from pans and cool completely on wire racks.

4. Beat the cream cheese in a medium bowl with an electric mixer on medium speed until it's smooth. Beat in the lemon curd. Stir in the whipped topping.

5. Spoon about **1 tablespoon** cheese mixture into each pastry cup. Refrigerate for at least 10 minutes before serving, or up to 1 day ahead. Top with a raspberry.   *Makes 24 tarts*

Thaw Time: 40 minutes • **Prep Time:** 10 minutes • **Bake Time:** 10 minutes
Cool Time: 30 minutes • **Chill Time:** 10 minutes

Lemon curd is made from lemon juice,
butter, egg yolks and sugar, a mixture that
thickens when cooked. Prepared lemon
curd can often be found in the supermarket
with the jams, jellies and preserves.

ACKNOWLEDGMENTS

The publisher would like to thank the companies and organizations listed below for the use of their recipes and photographs in this publication.

ACH Food Companies, Inc.

The Beef Checkoff

BelGioioso® Cheese Inc.

Bob Evans®

Cabot® Creamery Cooperative

Campbell Soup Company

ConAgra Foods, Inc.

Cream of Wheat® Cereal

Del Monte Foods

Dole Food Company, Inc.

EAGLE BRAND®

The Hershey Company

Jennie-O Turkey Store, LLC

Johnsonville Sausage, LLC

Kraft Foods Global, Inc.

MASTERFOODS USA

McIlhenny Company (TABASCO® brand Pepper Sauce)

Michael Foods, Inc.

Mrs. Dash® SALT-FREE SEASONING BLENDS

National Turkey Federation

Nestlé USA

North Dakota Wheat Commission

Ortega®, A Division of B&G Foods, Inc.

Reckitt Benckiser Inc.

Recipes courtesy of the Reynolds Kitchens

Riviana Foods Inc.

StarKist®

Stonyfield Farm®

Tyson Foods, Inc.

Unilever

U.S. Highbush Blueberry Council

Veg•All®

Wisconsin Milk Marketing Board